WAR AND DOMESTIC POLITICAL VIOLENCE

Volume 30, Sage Library of Social Research

SAGE LIBRARY OF SOCIAL RESEARCH

1. **DAVID CAPLOVITZ:** The Merchants of Harlem
2. **JAMES N. ROSENAU:** International Studies and the Social Sciences
3. **DOUGLAS E. ASHFORD:** Ideology and Participation
4. **PATRICK J. McGOWAN and HOWARD B. SHAPIRO:** The Comparative Study of Foreign Policy
5. **GEORGE A. MALE:** The Struggle for Power
6. **RAYMOND TANTER:** Modelling and Managing International Conflicts
7. **ANTHONY JAMES CATANESE:** Planners and Local Politics
8. **JAMES RUSSELL PRESCOTT:** Economic Aspects of Public Housing
9. **F. PARKINSON:** Latin America, the Cold War, and the World Powers, 1945-1973
10. **ROBERT G. SMITH:** Ad Hoc Governments
11. **RONALD GALLIMORE, JOAN WHITEHORN BOGGS, and CATHIE JORDAN:** Culture, Behavior and Education
12. **HOWARD W. HALLMAN:** Neighborhood Government in a Metropolitan Setting
13. **RICHARD J. GELLES:** The Violent Home
14. **JERRY L. WEAVER:** Conflict and Control in Health Care Administration
15. **GEBHARD LUDWIG SCHWEIGLER:** National Consciousness in Divided Germany
16. **JAMES T. CAREY:** Sociology and Public Affairs
17. **EDWARD W. LEHMAN:** Coordinating Health Care
18. **CHARLES G. BELL and CHARLES M. PRICE:** The First Term
19. **CLAYTON P. ALDERFER and L. DAVE BROWN:** Learning from Changing
20. **L. EDWARD WELLS and GERALD MARWELL:** Self-Esteem
21. **ROBERT S. ROBINS:** Political Institutionalization and the Integration of Elites
22. **WILLIAM R. SCHONFELD:** Obedience and Revolt
23. **WILLIAM C. McCREADY and ANDREW M. GREELEY:** The Ultimate Values of the American Population
24. **F. IVAN NYE:** Role Structure and Analysis of the Family
25. **PAUL WEHR and MICHAEL WASHBURN:** Peace and World Order Systems
26. **PATRICIA R. STEWART:** Children in Distress
27. **JUERGEN DEDRING:** Recent Advances in Peace and Conflict Research
28. **MOSHE M. CZUDNOWSKI:** Comparing Political Behavior
29. **JACK D. DOUGLAS:** Investigative Social Research
30. **MICHAEL STOHL:** War and Domestic Political Violence

War and Domestic Political Violence

The American Capacity for Repression and Reaction

MICHAEL STOHL

Preface by TED ROBERT GURR

Volume 30
SAGE LIBRARY OF
SOCIAL RESEARCH

 SAGE PUBLICATIONS   Beverly Hills   London

To my daughters
Rachel Jennifer and Ilene Sara

Copyright © 1976 by Sage Publications, Inc.

All rights reserved. No part of this book may be reproduced or utilized in any form or by any means, electronic or mechanical, including photocopying, recording, or by any information storage and retrieval system, without permission in writing from the publisher.

For information address:

SAGE PUBLICATIONS, INC.  SAGE PUBLICATIONS LTD
275 South Beverly Drive   St George's House / 44 Hatton Garden
Beverly Hills, California 90212   London EC1N 8ER

Printed in the United States of America

Library of Congress Cataloging in Publication Data

Stohl, Michael, 1947–
 War and domestic political violence.

 (Sage library of social research; v. 30)
 Bibliography: p. 145
 1. Violence—United States—History.   2. United States—Politics and government—20th century.
 3. Violence. I. Title.
 HN90.V5S86   301.6'33'0973   76-22799
 ISBN 0-8039-0575-0
 ISBN 0-8039-0576-9 pbk.

FIRST PRINTING

CONTENTS

Chapter		Page
	Preface by Ted Robert Gurr	1
1	Introduction to the Study of Linkages Between War and Domestic Political Violence in the United States	5
2	Toward a Knowledge Base for the Study of Political Violence Within Nations, or: Understanding Political Violence Made Difficult	11
3	Theory and Method in Studies of the Relationship Between Foreign and Domestic Violence	35
4	The Political System: Stratification and Patterns of Conflict and Violence	47
5	Research Design and the Construction of Indicators	67
6	American Violence in Historical Perspective: Reaction, Repression and the Maintenance of the American Political System	79
7	The Impact of War on Domestic Political Violence	97
8	Assessments, Extensions and Intensions of the Study of External-Internal Violence Linkages	123
	Appendix I: Tests of Significance	133
	Appendix II: Sample Code Sheet	137
	Appendix III: Statistical Data	139
	Bibliography	145
	About the Author	153

ACKNOWLEDGMENTS

Prefaces traditionally follow the format of indicating when and why a project was initiated and most importantly the people who were instrumental in its completion. In the course of completing this work I have learned why.

The actual initiation and completion of this work have benefited from the encouragement, assistance and patience of a large number of individuals. My foremost intellectual debt is owed to Ted Gurr, who from dissertation proposal through the generous assessment in the foreword surpassed what anyone may reasonably expect or hope for in scholar, teacher and friend. Not only was he encouraging and sympathetic during the long months of data collection and analysis but also quickly responsive, particularly during the year spent in London when distance could easily have slowed interactions. Most importantly, in a project that was at least by implication and often explication at odds with his own work, he demonstrated a laudable ability to discuss criticisms and to strengthen arguments that I had thought quite acceptable as they were.

My cohorts at Northwestern generated an exciting and challenging environment. In particular, I gratefully acknowledge the assistance of Peter Grabosky, who I involved at every stage and who at all times joyfully responded with helpful advice, and Raymond Duvall who aided me in the formulation of my proposal and the crucial early stages of data analysis.

Michael Nicholson of the Richardson Institute for Conflict and Peace Research provided me with much more than an office during my stay in London and the Woodrow Wilson Dissertation Fellowship made my travel to and stay in London possible. Peter Fairbrother, now of the University of Warwick, helped sharpen my appreciation of Marx and Weber during my year abroad. Jim Caporaso, John Paden, Donald Strickland, Arthur Stein, Bill Shaffer, Fred Homer, Michael McGrath and Ken Friedman critically evaluated early drafts, thereby making later drafts more cogent, and Quentin Davis provided assistance in the data analysis.

A special thanks is due Rhoda Blecker, of Sage Publications, who with untold patience and care guided the manuscript through the mysterious process of production.

My wife Cynthia was involved in every aspect of my progress. She labored in the Northwestern and University of London libraries, collecting much of the necessary data which made our trip to London feasible. The working environment she provided at all times is responsible more than anything else for the successful completion of my work.

PREFACE

This study challenges in some conceptual and theoretical ways a half-dozen intellectual conventions and empirical traditions in the quantitative study of political violence within nations. Professor Stohl rejects the convention by which the state's role in initiating many incidents of violence is ignored or dismissed as conflict management by an impartial arbiter. Instead he treats government agencies as partisans and analyzes their pro-system violence and that of other groups, side by side with anti-system violence. This set of distinctions—more elaborate than suggested here—follows from his more basic assumptions about the nature of internal conflict. Social, economic, and political groups in the United States, and in other societies, are assumed to occupy hierarchic positions in various stratification systems. Group violence is a recurrent tactic by which low-status groups have attempted to improve, and high-status groups have defended, their positions.

Having laid this conceptual groundwork, the author introduces the variable of international conflict, whose alleged impact on internal conflict has been the object of much previously inconsistent and unconvincing research. Theory and evidence on such "linkages" between internal and international conflict, when joined with assumptions about stratification systems, provide the ingredients for a specific theory about the domestic effects of warfare. Depending on its nature and success, war is likely to change the relative positions of contending groups, giving rise as the immediate aftermath of war, to intensified violence aimed especially at restoring the pre-war status quo.

These arguments will not be to everyone's taste. Some are made sketchily and less explicitly than one might wish. Moreover, by eschewing conventional ideologies about the role of the state in a plural democracy, the argument may seem to err in other ideological directions. Such doubts should be held in abeyance, because this is not "theory for theory's sake." Its proof lies in the results of the empirical work designed to test it.

On the methodological front Professor Stohl breaks with the "event" tradition of conflict analysis and asks not only the easy question of "how many events" but the more fundamental ones of what groups did what to whom, with what issues in mind, and with what intensity. Moreover he does so not in cross-section but instead with data spanning an eighty-year period for one country. The last five wars in which the United States has fought are represented, from the Spanish-American War through Vietnam. In each case his data depict, month by month, the incidence and magnitude of violent conflict by different groups during the years before, during, and (except for Vietnam) after each war. There are two possible grounds for criticism here. One is the reliance on the New York *Times* as the principal data source. On this issue one must agree with the author's point that no other comprehensive source is available. Also in his favor is the fact that these data are interpreted in the context of the historical literature on the subject. A second point of controversy may be that a priori assumptions are made about whether groups are pro- or anti-system solely on the basis of their structural position.

The statistical techniques used to analyze the data on internal conflict will be unfamiliar to many if not most readers. They were pioneered by psychologist Donald Campbell and go by the mouth-filling title of "quasi-experimental interrupted time-series analysis." The question they are designed to answer is a simple but important one and is beyond the capacity of ordinary correlation and regression analysis. It is whether the occurrence of some external event—the outbreak of war, in this study—works a significant change in the trend or magnitude of some continuous variable. Here the variables are measures of the frequency and magnitude of conflict by different groups over different issues. Since many measures are used, and many tests applied to each of them, it is sometimes difficult to pick out the general pattern of results from the mosaic of tabular and textual detail. But a general pattern *does* emerge, and it is one of considerable import both for theory and for our understanding of recent American history.

Suffice it to say here that all five wars prove to have had a substantial impact on the pattern of internal violence in the United States. While there have been considerable differences in the precise nature of the effects, in all cases the magnitude of violence increased significantly between the pre- and post-war periods, most consistently in violence initiated by government agencies in defense of the system. Professor Stohl interprets these results in their historical context and suggests that they are an integral part of the concerted efforts made to stifle dissent after both world wars. He also suggests that they help account for the abortive policies followed by the Nixon Administration in the waning years of the Vietnam war.

Professor Stohl contends that his results support the general theory proposed here. Others may want to suggest alternative or supplementary explanations, and Stohl is the first to acknowledge that further empirical work is required, especially in other societies. But the results he has achieved in this book appear as incontrovertable as they are exceptional. For the present, the burden of disproof rests with those who are sufficiently discomfited by Professor Stohl's theory to devise and test others. Whatever may come of such efforts, the present study must be counted as a provocative and innovative contribution to the systematic analysis of group conflict in general and in American history specifically.

May 1976 *Ted Robert Gurr*
Cambridge, England

Chapter 1

INTRODUCTION TO THE STUDY OF LINKAGES BETWEEN WAR AND DOMESTIC POLITICAL VIOLENCE IN THE UNITED STATES

When this work began more than four years ago, Watergate merely referred to a high-class Washington, D.C., apartment and office complex with some unusual architecture and a number of famous residents. As this work progressed, the nature of that referent obviously altered. The basic significance of the Watergate events and resultant investigations revolves around the description of the "climate" of the highest circles of government as revealed by a number of witnesses appearing before the Senate Committee, and the Constitutional arguments raised primarily by John Wilson, counsel for H. R. Haldeman and John Erlichman. The investigations concerned the government's duty to uphold the basic nature of the American social system or, consistent with the dominant sociological image, its equilibrium. This climate and the resultant legal colloquy appear to stem from the principle that the government is the political organization which is responsible for the relation of men dominating men, a relation supported by means of legitimate (i.e., *considered* legitimate) violence. The men in authority obviously considered their acts necessary and legitimate, although they admitted the risk that these acts might later prove embarrassing from a public relations standpoint and that their full disclosure might cause them to be misunderstood.

Watergate is not used to introduce this work merely because it is current and will make the work more "relevant" or important. Rather, the Watergate disclosures support a number of hypotheses concerning the impact of war on American domestic violence and the government's role in that relationship. Is Watergate and all it has come to signify an aberration or merely a recurrent response dressed up in new garb? The latter, in light of the evidence to be presented herein, is a much more likely assessment.

It has become rather commonplace when writing about violence in America to suggest that Americans suffer from what Graham and Gurr (1969: 788-822) call historical amnesia or others have called a repression of violence in the national consciousness (Hofstadter, 1970). Although reasons for this amnesia may be quite complex, there is clearly a conceptual blinder which assists the repression. American scholars generally consider the federal government an instrument which protects the community from violence, although the greatest and most calculating of killers is the national state, not only in international wars but in domestic conflict (Hofstadter, 1970: 6). The sources of this conceptual problem are in the distinction between government (with its political structure) and society at large. The use of physical force has been regarded by many writers as a characteristic and, hence, by implication, a legitimate feature of the political structure. Following Weber, we may identify the state as "a relation of men dominating men, a relation supported by means of legitimate [i.e., *considered* legitimate] violence" (Gerth and Mills, 1958: 78). A government is thereby identified with the legitimate use of force, and it becomes natural to dismiss governmental violence because it is simply viewed as normal. Research on violence within societies has generally, therefore, concentrated on "abnormal violence," or what is commonly referred to as civil strife. However, civil strife is not necessarily violent, and may simply refer to protests, demonstrations, or strikes which contain no actual physical attacks by one person on another. On the other hand, violent action by governmental agencies does not necessarily imply civil strife and in fact is frequently ignored by researchers who have most often been interested in why men rebel rather than why there is violence within a society or group of societies.

To approach the study of violence in this manner is consistent with the dominant paradigm of American social science, which sees conflict as an aberration and posits an equilibrium model of society as its "normal" state (see Parsons, 1951; for a further development of this point, see Coser, 1956: ch. 1; Buckley, 1967: ch. 2). An alternative model of social systems is the conflict model, which has been more influential in European thought than in American.

Dahrendorf has incisively contrasted the equilibrium model with the conflict model of society. He suggests (1959: 161) that, in the equilibrium model:

(1) Every society is a relatively persistent, stable structure of elements.
(2) Every society is a well integrated structure of elements.
(3) Every element in a society has a function—i.e., renders a contribution to its maintenance as a system.
(4) Every functioning social structure is based on a consensus of value among its members.

The Conflict model, on the contrary, posits:

(1) Every society is at every point subject to processes of change; social change is ubiquitous.
(2) Every society displays at every point dissensus and conflict; social conflict is ubiquitous.
(3) Every element in a society renders a contribution to its disintegration and change.
(4) Every society is based on the coercion of some of its members by others (1959: 162).

The ideological implications of the two models are not obscure. The equilibrium model, by stressing integration and consensus, leads directly to the position that conflict, which is a threat to stability, must be curtailed in order for the integration of the social structure to be maintained. Thus, government, which has the organizational task of maintenance, legitimately functions to suppress conflict, albeit only in response to disequilibrating aberrations. Hence, the ends of system maintenance justify the means. Contrarywise, the conflict model, which sees equilibrium as abnormal and only resulting from coercion, posits conflict as a normal, necessary, and continuing aspect of social systems. This model, then, sees societies as maintained by coercion and not by consensus among members.

In this study we will approach the analysis of American society within a general systems framework. A general systems approach, unlike the equilibrium model, views tension as a normal aspect of social relations and societies as complex adaptive systems. Hazlewood (1973: 4-6) has expressed three of its basic assumptions. First, all social systems are open, and "open systems engage in environment-system exchange which are an essential factor underlying the system's viability, its reproductive ability or continuity, and its ability to change." Second, complex adaptive systems are tension-oriented; tension is assumed to be the basis and perpetuator of the society. Finally,

> Complex adaptive systems are inherently structure elaborating and changing, they react to the stimuli in their environment by elaborating or changing their structure to a higher or more complex level.

The general systems framework thus implies a tendency toward adaptation and mutual responsiveness to interactions and resultant changes in system states. We will thus avoid the bias of prejudging governmental violence as legitimate and instead explore how government and the American people react to changes in their social, economic, and political environment.

In Chapter 2, we will discuss a number of approaches and studies seeking to explain the sources of conflict, aggression, and violence. The major causes of violence are discussed primarily in terms of either individual goal frustrations and resultant aggression (normally equated directly with violence) and the structural conditions—incompatibility of interests, and the political-philosophical differences—which lead to direct physical violence. As such, we are primarily concerned with examining the literature on manifest direct personal violence (see Galtung, 1969) and not with structural or indirect violence. However, a few words should be said in relation to structural violence.

There are two basic directions an emphasis on structural violence can take. The first would maintain that violence need not necessarily be overt to be acknowledged. For example, any system which prevented one class or section of its membership from enjoying economic, cultural, social, or political benefits available to others is, in effect, committing violence to that section. The second would concentrate only on the type of structural conditions which would lead or have led to direct physical violence. For the most part, researchers have been concerned with the latter aspects of structural violence and we will also be primarily concerned with direct rather than indirect violence—not because a consideration of structural violence in terms of the former direction is unimportant, but rather because my own interest lies primarily with the latter. In future work, the two directions may well be integrated into a full theory of the causes of violence.

As we shall see in Chapter 2, much of the work on violence within national societies has ignored the impact of the external environment and the state's response to that environment. Thus, in Chapter 3, we will explore studies of the relationship between internal and external violence to discover any possible linkages and fruitful lines of inquiry. One of the conclusions of Chapter 3 is that the study of the interaction between domestic and international systems must use a conceptual framework which is conducive to the study of linkages.

The framework in Chapter 4 assumes that the political system distributes values within a social system. My approach, consistent with a specific orientation in group conflict theory, uses as its basic premise "that violent conflict and revolution arise out of group conflicts over valued conditions and positions" (Gurr, 1971a: 12). The chapter outlines the major structures and interactions in the domestic system of the United States and discusses how and with what effects violence in the environment (especially inputs from the international system) is likely to alter the system's internal structures and interactions.

Chapter 5 introduces the quasi-experimental interrupted time series design which will be used to test the hypotheses suggested in the previous chapters. This design is both necessary and appropriate, as it allows for the introduction of the independent variable (war) at specified times in the sequence of events. Problems of the design's limitations are also discussed. As a result of felt inadequacies with existing data sets, as indicated in Chapters 2 and 3, it was necessary to develop a new data set and construct appropriate indicators of domestic violence. The procedure for this collection as well as likely trouble spots and confounding variables are also discussed in this chapter.

The sixth chapter presents the results of the data collection concerning the general pattern of domestic violence in the United States in the prewar and postwar years contained in the period 1890-1970. The discussion includes the distribution of violence by type, participants and initiators, and the magnitude and intensity for each type of political violence. In addition, the chapter highlights the role of government agencies in violence events. The discussion of types also takes cognizance of the changes in type, magnitude, and intensity with the passage of time.

Chapter 7 contains the results of the interrupted time series analyses for each of the five wars which occurred in the time period under study, and a comparative discussion then evaluates the hypotheses generated in Chapter 4 in light of these results. The concluding chapter discusses the theoretical framework and methodological approach of the research in terms of their demonstrated usefulness and limitations. The book concludes with suggestions as to additional research avenues and some new conjectures as to the relationship between war and domestic political violence.

Chapter 2

TOWARD A KNOWLEDGE BASE FOR THE STUDY OF POLITICAL VIOLENCE WITHIN NATIONS, OR: UNDERSTANDING POLITICAL VIOLENCE MADE DIFFICULT

Introduction

Much time and effort has been spent in attempts at explaining the phenomenon of political violence. People in authority see violence perpetrated by those who are not "legitimate" power holders as disruptive and hence dangerous to the continuance of authority. Those either seeking authoritative positions or attempting to rid themselves of another's authority often see violence as an efficient means to secure their goals. Both those who employ violence and those who attempt to limit it—often the same individuals—seek explanations of when, where, how, and why violence occurs.

The following adds to a growing literature searching for such explanations and guided by an explicit philosophy of inquiry which asserts that the proper question in the growth of knowledge should not be the source of knowledge, but rather, "How can we hope to detect and eliminate error?" To answer that question, Popper suggests, we must criticize our own errors as well. Knowledge thus increases not by verifying theories, but by attempting to disprove them.

> The criterion of the scientific status of a theory is its falsifiability, or refutability, or testability [Popper, 1969: 36-37].

The main objective of this chapter is to generate the knowledge base concerning the causes of political violence within societies required for an understanding of the relationship between the internal and external violent behavior of nations. We will review attempts to explain the sources of political violence within nations, to highlight the shortcomings of theories of violence and to discover some of the requirements of a new theory of political violence.

The great volume of material on this subject allows an eclectic rather than a comprehensive review. I have thus chosen examples to illustrate a number of problems believed to be common to studies concerning political violence. The varied backgrounds of the different researchers who have ventured explanations is reflected in the variety of approaches to the study of political violence. Sociologists, economists, and political scientists have most often studied violence within a perspective which is commonly referred to as a conflict theory approach. Conflict theorists are generally concerned with the incompatibility of interests, structural conditions and constraints, and philosophical bases of political systems. Biologists and psychologists, on the other hand, have anchored their research efforts in explanations of aggressive behavior, which are normally concerned with the physiological bases of aggression, the roles of frustration and learning theory, and the problems of cognitive dissonance. In addition, there have been a number of attempts to synthesize approaches across either levels or disciplines with varying, often disappointing, results.

This review will focus around the following questions with a specific interest in operationalizing variables in the latter part of the research:

(1) What is the underlying model of the political system?

(2) What are the possible types of conflict, conflict behavior, aggression, and violence that occur within the system?

(3) How and why would conflict behavior, aggression, or violence occur?

(4) What are the parameters of the explanations offered, and to what types of systems and to what levels of analysis are they applicable?

Conflict Theory and the Study of Political Violence

In 1908, Georg Simmel anticipated much of this century's work in the study of conflict. An analysis of his essay "Conflict" (1955) provides a useful base for the understanding of conflict and the problems involved endeavoring such an understanding. Simmel established no formal theory from which testable hypotheses are deduced. Rather, he explicated his assumptions and subsequent insights as he wove the fabric of his essay from form to content. As a result, he moved very freely between pure forms and particular cases, and it is difficult to paraphrase his insights without losing much of the richness and subtlety of their meaning.

The basic purpose of the essay is to establish the positive sociological significance of conflict. To this purpose, Simmel (1955: 13) asks: "Is conflict a form of sociation?"

> If every interaction among men is a sociation, conflict—after all one of the most vivid interactions, which furthermore cannot possibly be carried on by one individual alone—must certainly be considered as sociation.

Simmel further argues that conflict is a positive force within groups and a necessary part of the social process, and that dissociative factors are the cause of conflict. Thus, conflict has as a basic function the resolution of these divisions. "Conflict is thus designed to resolve divergent dualisms; it is a way of achieving some kind of unity, even it be through the annihilation of one of the conflicting parties" (1955: 13).

Conflicting patterns are thus not something to be automatically avoided or minimized but, contrariwise, may have positive benefits. The group, the principal sociological entity, is thus placed in a new perspective, for it is seen as constituted not only by harmonious but also by antagonistic relationships. Hostility and opposition are presented as principal components of sociation. Opposition is not "only a means for preserving the relation but one of the concrete functions which actually constitute it" (Simmel, 1955: 19). Conflict and cooperation both have positive social functions and are both conditions necessary to the social structure. Conflict acts as an integrative force in the group and determines its form. Conflicting relationships, combined with unifying forces, produce the social structure and together they constitute the group as a concrete, living unit.

Simmel also posits hostility as a primary characteristic of human nature. He reminds the reader of how much easier it is to inspire hostility than confidence or sympathy in a relationship.

> This instinct of opposition emerges with the inevitability of a reflex movement, even in quite harmonious relationships in very conciliatory persons.... It would mean that the first instinct with which the individual affirms himself is the negation of the other [Simmel, 1955: 29].

The introduction of hostility as a primary force in sociation leads to a distinction between two types of conflict, which Coser (1956: 49) labels realistic and nonrealistic. The two forms can be seen as derived from Tonnies' (1963) Kurwille and Wesenwille, the rational and natural will. Realistic conflict in its pure form derives from a rational approach to a situation.

> If the conflict is caused by an object, by the will to have or control something, it is qualified by the fact that in principle every end can be attained by more than one means. The desire for possession or subjugation, even for the annihilation of the enemy can be satisfied through combinations other than fight [Simmel, 1955: 27].

Nonrealistic conflict, on the other hand, derives from the Wesenwille.

> It is exclusively determined by subjective feelings where there are inner energies which can be satisfied only through fight, its substitution by other means is impossible; it is its own purpose and context and hence wholly free from the admixture of other forms of relation [Simmel, 1955: 27-28].

The two designated forms are viewed as pure types that do not appear as separate realities but that may be observed in combination. Thus, in every conflict, we must recognize that the purity of conflict for its own sake is always interspersed with more objective interests and that "no serious conflict probably lasts any length of time without being sustained by a complex of psychological impulses" (Simmel, 1955: 34).

Realistic conflict, furthermore, contains within it the phenomenon of competition, a form of sociation where conflict is indirect. Competition is distinguished by the following properties: it is conflict which consists of parallel efforts by both parties to obtain the same prize, the outcome does not constitute the goal, and the competitor does not use his strength on the adversary but rather aims at the goal. In addition,

> Competition is usefully thought of as a special case of conflict in which the parties to conflict have already subscribed to another common value or set of values, which is superordinate to the values in conflict and which transfer satisfaction otherwise derived by the individual realizing the scarce value in question into satisfaction derived from the resolution of the competition [Stevenson, 1971: 52].

Victory in the competition is not the success of the competition but the realization of values outside it. The most common example suggested is the case of two runners competing in a race, where the scarce value is being first over the finish line; it is competition as long as one player does not prevent—except by running faster—the other player from finishing first.

It is from this form of conflict that most modern students of conflict theory begin their analyses. Realistic group conflict theory and game theory generally concern themselves with the conflict between groups engaged in competition which results from some objective difference between the groups. Boulding's (1964) concepts of conflict are typical of this approach, seeing conflict as any "change in the position of the social universe that makes one party better off and another worse off." Another work of Boulding's (1962) describes conflict "as a situation of competition in which the parties are aware of the incompatibility of potential future positions and in which each party wishes to occupy a position that is incompatible with the other." Jesse Barnard (1957) claims that

> conflict exists between groups when there is a fundamental incompatibility in their values, goals, and interests so that if one group gets what it wants, the other group cannot get what it wants. Conflict so conceived can exist independently of the subjective reactions of members of the groups.

This ignores the importance of the distinction between Simmel's two ideal types and raises a few problems for analysts of conflict. Who, for instance, decides the existence of the incompatibility and how would they avoid the problem of dealing with individuals in social situations and not merely social structures? Simmel himself is guilty of this emphasis, for, having raised the distinction as one ideal type and then taken the time to distinguish between hostility and its role in conflict, he discusses only conflict and competition of the realistic type in the remainder of the essay. Lewis Coser has made propositions of a number of Simmel's more important assertions, which indicate the role of conflict in the formation and maintenance of the group and its social structure. Some of the propositions are:

(1) Conflict serves to establish and maintain the identity and boundary lines of societies and groups.

(2) Conflict with other groups contributes to the establishment and reaffirmation of the identity of the group and maintains its boundaries against the surrounding social world.

(3) Conflict with other groups leads to the mobilization of the energies of the group members and hence to increased cohesion of the group.

A parallel argument is discussed by Sumner (1906: 12)

> The relation of comradeship and peace in the we-group and that of hostility and war toward other-groups are correlatives to each other. The exigencies of war with outsiders are what makes peace inside, lest outsiders are what makes peace inside, lest internal discord should weaken the we-group for war. These exigencies also make government and law in the in-group, in order to prevent quarrels and enforce discipline. Thus war and peace have reacted on each other and developed

each other, one within the group, the other in the intergroup relation. The closer the neighbors, and the stronger they are, the intenser is the warfare, and then the intenser is the internal organization and discipline of each.

These propositions introduce another problem. This concerns the impact of other groups on the structure and interactions of the original group. Simmel, Coser, and Sumner suggest that conflict with other groups will increase the internal cohesion of a group. They neglect, however, to distinguish the level and type of conflict that will produce such increased cohesion. Will threats suffice? Or must the group resort to war? Simmel states that, in short: the group in a state of peace can permit antagonistic members within it to live with one another in an undecided situation because each of them can go his own way and avoid collisions. "A state of conflict pulls the members of a group so tightly together that they must either get completely along with or completely repel one another" (Simmel, 1955: 92-93).

Consistent with Simmel, Fanon, in his tract *The Wretched of the Earth* (1963: 93), advocated the use of violence to create united communities.

> But it so happens that for the colonized people this violence, because it constitutes their only work, invests their characters with positive and creative qualities. The practice of violence binds them together as a whole.... The groups recognize each other and the future nation is already indivisible.

Was this what Simmel had in mind?

Clearly, these authors are referring to two different aspects of conflict—Simmel referring to the situation rather than the act of conflict, Fanon concerned with the act. This introduces the problem of differences between conflict of interest and conflict behavior. Conflict of interest refers to the way in which the preferences of the parties in a sociation are related, and thus to the structure of the situation in which they find themselves and each other. It does not refer to the behavior of the parties in a conflict of interest situation. It is not clear from Simmel's work if the impact of this proposition would be changed if both conceptual aspects of conflict were considered. This is not an uncommon problem in the literature of conflict theory, and we will return to it later.

Dahrendorf (1959: 213) has raised another issue which we might consider. He suggests that the process of conflict behavior involves two contributing variables—the intensity of behavior and the instrumental aspects of behavior. Intensity of behavior refers "to the energy expenditure and degree of involvement of conflicting parties... the more importance the individual participants of a conflict attach to its issues and substance the more intense is this conflict."

The instrumental aspect of a conflict relates to the type of weapon (threats, violence, boycott) the parties choose to employ in expressing their conflict behavior. Does the choice of violent behavior change the character of the situation? Does it merely intensify the impact of the conflict on the group? Or does it indicate the intensity of the conflict for the group? Weber (1947: 133) was of the opinion that "the treatment of conflict involving the use of physical violence as a separate type is justified by the special characteristics of the employment of this means and the corresponding consequences of its use." Thus, we must differentiate between the type of conflict behavior chosen in order for us to detect whether it changes the nature of the sociation.

In Coser's third proposition, it is posited that conflict with other groups increases internal cohesion. How might one measure increases in cohesion? Cohesion commonly refers to the harmonious interconnections of entities in a group. Thus, it is concerned with the bringing together of separate parts into a whole. In studies of intersocietal relations, this concept is often known as integration. A common approach has been to define integration as some possibility that conflict within a community might be resolved without violence (Deutsch et al., 1957; North, 1968). Integration or cohesion thus often indicate the extent and intensity of violence in the community. A cohesive community would be a social unit in which "there is likelihood of internal peaceful change in a setting of groups with mutually antagonistic claims" (Haas, 1961).

Conceptualizing cohesion in this manner and distinguishing among types of conflict behavior permits the solution of an apparent paradox in Simmel's work. Simmel has said that conflict with outside groups results in cohesion within the group. One tends to conclude that levels of conflict within the group should decrease. However, Simmel asserts that the absence of conflict cannot serve as an indicator of the group's underlying cohesion. Rather, he states that the closer any relationship is, the more likely conflict is to be expressed without fear of the group's disintegration. This would appear to follow from his earlier point that opposition and hostility are normal and positive aspects of sociation. However, the proposition is important. If one distinguishes between types of conflict behavior, the paradox is solved by interpreting Simmel as indicating that, in cohesive groups, violent or destructive conflict would decrease, while conflict behavior involving positive manifestations of conflict should increase.

A caveat to this proposition states that if conflict with another group defines the group's structure and may achieve some unity, there are a number of assumptions that must be met. If the group is lacking in basic consensus, conflict with an outside group may lead to the group's disintegration. However, if the conflict concerns goals, values, or interests that contradict the basic assumptions upon which the group is founded, and the group is characterized by a basic consensus, conflict will have positive effects (as in Great Britain in 1914). When interpreting the result of the interaction between the group under study and other groups, the researcher must be concerned with how the environment reflects the internal structure and its cleavages.

Simmel also discusses "the search for enemies." Leaders of groups faced with the threat of disintegration may find it useful to establish enemies that will serve to remind the group of the need for unity as vital to their existence (Hitler's use of both internal and external enemies being the most notorious example). This search for enemies and the resultant conflict is a familiar theme in the literature of international relations. Haas and Whiting (1956) suggest that groups seeking self-preservation may be driven to a foreign policy of conflict: "In times of extreme domestic tension among elites, a policy of uniting a badly divided nation against some real or alleged outside threat frequently seems useful to a ruling group" (Haas and Whiting, 1956: 62). Similarly, Rosecrance (1963) suggests that there is a tendency for international instability to be associated with the domestic insecurity of elites. He argues: "There may be other reasons for commencement of hostilities, but internal instability seems to be closely connected with the major destabilizing military transformation of modern times" (Rosecrance, 1963: 294). Clearly, the international system affects and is affected by the occurrence of conflict in the domestic system. Any theory of political violence must consider environmental impacts on the domestic system.

The main points of these arguments, with the modifications suggested, are as follows:

(1) Conflict is a mutual act which is a principal component in the determination of social structures.

(2) Conflict will tend to result in an increase in internal cohesion within groups. It is hypothesized that this cohesion will be manifested by decreases in violence within the group. An important gap in our knowledge is the difference in the effect conflict as an act and conflict as a situation will have on this relationship.

Three mediating variables have also been proposed for this hypothesis:

(a) the greater the external threat to the goals or values of the group, the stronger the relationship;

(b) the greater the pre-existing cohesion of the group, the stronger the relationship;

(c) the greater the instability of the group, the more likely it is to participate in conflict with other groups.

There still remain unanswered a number of the questions which were posed earlier in this review, and a few additional problems have been raised as a result of looking at the conflict theorists' work. The first, the effects of interaction with the environment, will be discussed in Chapter 3. The second basic issue concerns the role of political structures on the nature of conflict and resulting violence.

Political scientists explain that violence within systems generally takes place when political institutions break down or when regimes lose authority and legitimacy. These explanations assume that governments or the state possess, or should possess, the claim to the monopoly of force or violence (Parsons, 1964; Rose, 1971; Easton, 1953; Weber, 1947). The impetus for violence is therefore seen as resulting from attempts by those who deny this authority to challenge the monopoly. As a result, much of the literature that deals with the causes of violence identifies violence with insurgents and order with the regime. Questions thus asked concern the problems of shaping political institutions and mechanisms that will create or maintain order.

A most influential work within this perspective is Huntington's *Political Order in Changing Societies* (1968). Its primary thesis is that political instability and violence are in large part "the product of rapid social change and the rapid mobilization of new groups into politics coupled with the slow development of political institutions" (Huntington, 1968: 4). Political stability is dependent on the ability of societies and their governments to develop political institutions that can cope with the increases in participation that economic and social changes bring to a modernizing society. "The primary problem of politics is the lag in the development of political institutions behind social and economic change" (Huntington, 1968: 5). The primary structures for preventing this lag from developing are the political parties and party system.

> A society which develops reasonably well organized political parties while the level of political participation is still relatively low (as was largely the case in India, Uraguay, Chile, England, the United States and Japan) is likely to have a less destabilizing expansion of political participation than a society where parties are organized later in the process of modernization [Huntington, 1968: 398].

Strong political parties, he notes, require high levels of institutionalization and mass support. Is, then, political order synonymous with an institutionalized party system, or is the existence of the party system a precondition of political order? Even more fundamentally, is governmental authority dependent on political institutions or are political institutions dependent on governmental legitimacy as a condition of their development (Nardin, 1971: 37)?

Rose (1971) in his work on Northern Ireland posits that violence in general (and particularly in the special case of Northern Ireland) occurs because of the regime's lack of authority. If a regime can obtain high support and compliance it will create low potentials for violence. Conversely, if it has low support and compliance it will have high potentials for violence. The authority of regimes can be measured and differentiated by two characteristics: the extent of diffuse support for the regime among intended subjects, and the extent to which its population complies with basic political laws (Rose, 1971: 28).

We have defined domestic political violence as violence that takes place within the autonomous political system. However, within the boundaries of a single state more than one political system (a structure for allocating goods and services) may exist, and as Nardin (1971) discusses in general and Rose (1971) points out in the Northern Ireland case, there may exist structures that compete for authority within the system. Violence may result from opposing forces attempting to impose their authority on the subjects.

Thus, violence in practical terms becomes a rational instrument in the pursuit of political goals. Political instability therefore becomes

> a condition in political systems in which the institutionalized patterns of authority break down, and the expected compliance to political authorities is replaced by violence intended to change the personnel, policies or sovereignty of the political authorities by injury to persons or property [Stevenson, 1971: 7].

Violence in these studies is seen as resulting from an "objective" or rational assessment of the political conditions within society and the need to either obtain or maintain compliance with authority. But what mechanisms are responsible for the making of such an assessment? For this answer we must turn to the psychologists and biologists and their discussions of the determinants of aggressive behavior.

Aggression and Violence

The frustration-aggression hypothesis has played a major role in theories about the conditions necessary for the occurrence of political violence. DeTocqueville's (1954) observations concerning the ancient regime and the origins of the French Revolution have greatly influenced present approaches to the problem. DeTocqueville's thesis, generally referred to as the "revolution in rising expectations," asserts that revolutions occur because of frustrated expectations during a period of improving social, economic, and political conditions. Three current proponents of this thesis, Davies, Gurr, and the Feierabends have expanded on the original argument. Davies has modified the thesis in his "J-Curve hypothesis." He asserts:

> [Revolutions] are most likely to occur when a prolonged period of objective economic and social development is followed by a short period of sharp reversal. The all important effect on the minds of the people in a particular society is to produce during the former period, an expectation of continued stability to satisfy needs—which continue to rise—and during the latter, a mental state of anxiety and frustration when manifest reality breaks away from anticipated reality. The actual state of socio-economic development is less significant than the expectation that past progress, now blocked, can and must continue in the future [Davies, 1969: 120].

Gurr takes a slightly different approach, but one that is consistent with the basic frustration-aggression hypothesis.

> The social-psychological potential for collective violence is a diffuse disposition toward aggressive action, a primary variable whose immediate determinant in a collectivity are the intensity and scope of relative deprivation. Relative deprivation is defined in psychological terms as a perceived discrepancy between men's value expectations and their value capabilities, i.e. a discrepancy between the goods and conditions they believe are their due, and the goods and conditions they think they can in fact get and keep [Gurr, 1970: 319].

The Feierabends (1966) have introduced the concept of systemic frustration as a source of political instability and violence. Systemic frustration is produced by interference with the attainment of social goals, aspirations, and values. Frustration is experienced simultaneously and collectively within societies. Violent political behavior is thus instigated by systemic frustration.

This concept illustrates what I believe to be an all too common problem of social theorists who attempt to combine levels of analysis. Because Gurr's study is most explicitly multilevel in its approach, it is the most vulnerable to this criticism. He has drawn the frustration-aggression hypothesis from psychological literature and employs it as the basic axiom in his theory of violence. A problem arises, however, because the empirical status of the relationship is not clear within the psychological literature itself. By placing this hypothesis as the crucial link in the causal framework of the theory, Gurr cannot empirically test the hypothesis itself. In this section we shall explore other plausible rival hypotheses of aggressive behavior and discuss their implications for the frustration-aggression hypothesis and Gurr's study (see Figure 2.1).

The first problem encountered in frustration-aggression literature is that there exists no agreed definition of the major concepts. The original formulation by Dollard et al. (1939: 9) defined aggression as a "sequence of behavior, the goal response to which is the injury of the person toward whom it is directed." Although the definition appears to refer to organism-directed responses, the Dollard group contended that the aggression need not be overt and could be directed (including symbolically) toward inanimate

---

We may diagram Gurr's theory of political violence in the following manner to illustrate the place of the different source and levels in the development of the theory.

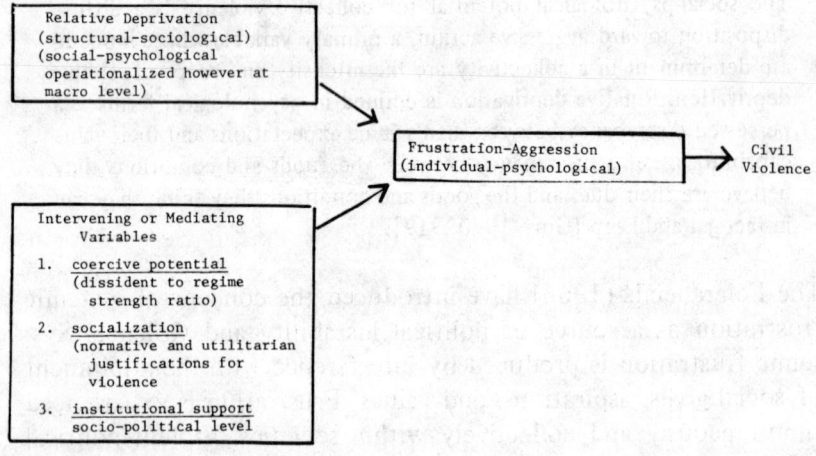

Figure 2.1: GURR: WHY MEN REBEL

objects as well. After much criticism of the concepts of aggression, Berkowitz (1969: 3), the leading exponent of the theory today, has refined the concept to "behavior whose goal response is the inflicting of injury on some object or persons. The behavior may be overt (physical or verbal) or implicit (as in the case of thoughts)." Buss, however, believes that these formulations are too broad. He would prefer to define aggression as "a response that delivers noxious stimuli to another organism" (Buss, 1961: 1). He feels that the inclusion of intent in definitions is both awkward and unnecessary. Instead he would prefer to consider reinforcing consequences that affect the occurrence and strength of aggressive responses. The two major reinforcers are angry aggression, stimulated by the victims suffering injury or pain, and instrumental aggression, stimulated by extrinsic rewards. It is interesting to note that most social conflict theorists make a similar distinction between types of conflict behavior, differentiating between realistic and unrealistic conflict, or rational and nonrational conflict behaviors (Coser, 1956; Schelling, 1960). Thus, the analysis of the studies that follow is complicated by the fact that there are different conceptual criteria considered in the operationalization of aggressive responses.

The concept of frustration is also not without its operational difficulties. The Dollard study (1939: 7) defined it as "interference with the occurrence of an instigated goal response at its proper time in the behavior sequence." Buss suggests that it be regarded as the blocking of any action typically leading to a reinforcer. Many different operationalizations have been suggested for producing frustration. Berkowitz suggests that this may account for the many failures to confirm the frustration-aggression relationship, rather than the hypothesis' lack of validity. In any case, until the formulation is placed within a design that allows for its negation, and the proper time in the behavior sequence is indicated, it appears that alternative explanations for the formulation's failure will be advanced.

Some studies of aggressive behavior do not appear to have frustration as their primary determinant. Many child and social psychologists suggest that aggressive behavior is primarily learned. Their studies emphasize the personality characteristics acquired during the socialization process. The stimuli to aggression in studies involving these theories of learning and development generally are referred to as reinforcements, disinhibitors, and modeling effects of aggressive behavior.

A number of studies have demonstrated that the observation of violence and aggressive behavior can increase the likelihood of subsequent aggressive behavior. Subjects have been shown films, cartoons, or aggressive adult models and then been placed in situations where they are given the opportunity to display aggressive behavior. Mussen and Rutherford (1961) showed aggressive cartoons to children, mildly frustrated them, and then placed them in a play situation. The results indicated that experimentally induced frustration had no influence on the incidence of aggression, although there was increased verbal aggression as a result of the exposure. Bandura, Ross and Ross (1961) exposed one group of nursery-school children to aggressive adult models who displayed their aggression toward a plastic doll; a second group was exposed to models who displayed nonaggressive behavior (they ignored the doll and sat quietly in the room), and a third group received no exposure to models and was studied as a control group. In the free play period that followed, the children who had witnessed the aggressive models displayed a great number of imitative aggressive responses. Such aggressive responses rarely occurred in the nonaggressive model group, although these responses were more frequent than in the control group. Bandura (1962) showed that there is a high probability of a child's displaying aggressive reaction to frustration only when he has learned aggression as a dominant response to a specific situation. He found that children who had observed a model behaving in an aggressive way and were then frustrated responded in an imitative manner, while equally frustrated children who had watched the nonaggressive model imitated their model's behavior, and exhibited less aggression than the control group. In a third experiment (Bandura, Ross and Ross, 1963) the authors included the effects of real-life models, human film aggression, and cartoon film aggression. Again the children were mildly frustrated. The results indicated that film mediated models were as effective as real life models in transmitting the same aggressive patterns of behavior.

There have been a number of other studies that indicate that children who are shown cartoons containing aggressive content and are then compared to control groups in various play situations will display a relatively high frequency of aggressive responses. Siegel (1956) used aggressive toys in a free play situation as the dependent variable, while Lovaas (1961a) studied the activation of a hitting response in a mechanical toy (a bobo doll). Larder (1962) found that tape recorded aggressive story material also produced increases in the children's aggressive behavior in a play situation involving the bobo doll.

The preceding experiments have all dealt with stimulating children to produce aggressive behavior. There have been a number of studies dealing with adult subjects. Walters and Thomas (1963) and Walters, Thomas and Acker (1962) requested that subjects assist the experimenter in a study of the effects of punishment on learning. As assistants, the subjects were required to deliver shocks to a confederate presented as another subject. After pretest trials the subjects viewed a scene from the movie, "Rebel Without a Cause," depicting a fight with switch blades. Control subjects viewed an educational film depicting adolescents engaged in constructive art work. The differences between the intensity levels of pretest and posttest shocks determined the experiment's effect. The experimenters found that, in general, the experimental group demonstrated a greater increase in the levels of shock administered. However, in the second study, where there was the additional control of the group's division into those with high and low inhibitions against shocking, the high inhibition subjects did not significantly increase the intensity of shock as a result of reinforcement, in comparison with high inhibition controls. The experimenters concluded that the initial level of aggression inhibition in adults influences the extent to which positive aggression reinforcement is demonstrated in overt behavior.

Berkowitz and Geen (1967: 364) contend that the series of Wisconsin studies have consistently found that "the aggression-heightening consequences of observed violence are detectable only when the subjects had previously been angered by the person they are later to attack." Thus Berkowitz and Rawlings (1963) found that when subjects who had previously viewed a film depicting justified aggression were insulted by a confederate of the experimenter, subjects' inhibitions were lowered, producing overt hostility toward the insulting confederate. Berkowitz and Geen

(1967) gave puzzle completions tasks to three groups of subjects each paired with a confederate. In every case the confederate was given a puzzle which he was able to complete. The subjects in one group were given insolvable puzzles which after five minutes were picked up by the experimenter who announced that the subject had not completed his puzzle, while the confederate had; in a second group the confederate insulted the subject for his inability to finish the puzzle; and in a third group the subject was given an easily solvable puzzle. The subjects were shown a film with either a fight scene or a one mile race. They were then given an opportunity to deliver electric shocks (as punishment in a learning situation) to the confederate introduced as Kirk (whose name corresponded to the victim's in the fight scene) or Bob. Emotionally aroused subjects exhibited stronger aggression toward the confederate named "Kirk" after witnessing the boxing movie because of the association of the target's name. This happened in both the task frustrating and the direct insult situations. It is important to note that the attack frustrating condition of verbal insult elicited no greater response than that of the mildly frustrating experience of not finishing the task. This lends support to the argument that modeling is the more important determinant of aggressive behavior.

Further support is provided by Hartmann (1969) who investigated the independent and interactive effects of anger instigation, aggressive display, and pain cues on subsequent interpersonal aggression. The dependent measures were the character and intensity of the shocks the subjects obstensibly administered to their provocateur. The experimenter revealed that regardless of arousal levels, the subjects who had witnessed the modeled aggression behaved more punitively than did subjects who had witnessed the same models behaving nonaggressively.

Experimentally induced positive reinforcement of aggressive behavior has also been shown to lead to an increase in aggression behavior following frustration. Walters and Brown (1963) reinforced children's aggressive behavior in play situations and then frustrated them. Davitz (1952) has shown that boys trained in aggressive responses showed relatively more aggression following frustration, while boys trained in constructive responses showed more constructiveness in their behavior. Patterson, Ludwig and

Sonada (1961) found that children who had been verbally reinforced for hitting an inflated doll were more aggressive with the doll in a subsequent session than children who had not been trained to respond aggressively.

Lovaas (1961b) has reported that children who were reinforced for aggressive verbal responses during a training period showed a marked increase in the number of aggressive responses, and children who were reinforced for nonaggressive verbal responses responded with an increase of nonaggressive behavior. But, in a posttraining period free play situation, the children reinforced for aggressive responses displayed greater aggressive behavior than children who had been reinforced for nonaggressive behavior.

Experiments with adult subjects have shown the same direction of responses. In a number of studies, subjects have been conditioned to emit greater frequencies of hostile statements or expressions (Binder, McConnell and Sjoholm, 1957; Buss and Durkee, 1958; Simkins, 1961; Zedek, 1959; Bandura, Lipsher and Miller, 1960; and Goldman, 1961). Moreover, the Milgram (1963) study has shown that reinforcement for aggression may come from obedience to authority figures for whom the subject may willingly or hesitantly administer shocks in the guise of a learning experiment, the reinforcement having acquired its power during the socialization process whereby one learns to obey authority figures. Interestingly, the Milgram experiment took place without the required frustration-aggression pattern.

Staples and Walters (1964) tested the effects of aggression reinforcement on subjects with high and low inhibitions to aggression as measured by the delivery of shocks to a confederate. The results of the verbal reinforcement for shock administration in the training indicated that, levels of shock delivery by low inhibited subjects increased to a greater extent than highly inhibited subjects, if levels of shock are taken as an index of inhibitors. This finding is consistent with the Walters and Thomas (1963) study.

The preceding discussion has dealt with experimentally induced antecedents of aggression. The discussion has demonstrated that aggression most consistently occurs as a result of modeling of imitative behavior, through the lowering of inhibitions, and through the positive reinforcement of aggressive behavior. The role of frustration emerges as an intervening variable in some studies and is nonoperative in others. There have been cases where frustration has had no effect in eliciting aggression and cases where it has served to intensify the elicited aggression. There have also been cases where aggression has occurred despite lack of frustrating antecedents.

Turning to the literature of correlational studies, there is a little more evidence for the frustration-aggression relationship. An author of the original frustration-aggression study working with an associate (Hovland and Sears, 1940) hypothesized that economic frustrations would correlate with aggressive behavior. They chose cotton prices as the basis for their economic index and found a strong negative correlation (−.67) between the index and southern lynchings over a period of forty-nine years. However, when their data were reanalyzed by Mintz (1946), he found that statistical artifacts had been responsible for the correlation and that there was no relationship between the two phenomena.

Henry and Short (1954), in their work on homicide and suicide, assume much of the same conceptual framework that Hovland and Sears employed. Henry and Short postulate that downtrends in the economic cycle frustrate one's ability to maintain a constant or rising position in a status hierarchy and that more aggressive behavior should occur during such periods. Data are introduced to show that homicide and aggravated assault are correlated with fluctuations in the business cycle.

The relationship between parents' use of punishment (considered as blocking of an instigated goal response) toward aggressive behavior in their children, has been examined in a number of studies. Sears, Whiting, Howliss, and Sears (1953) have reported that mothers who moderately frustrate and punish aggression have children who display high interpersonal aggression in nursery school. They report less aggression from children whose mothers report either very light or very severe punishment. Sears, Maccoby, and Levin (1957) conclude that there is a clear positive correlation in boys between severity of maternal punishment for aggression and amount of overt aggression shown by the child in preschool, and that there is a slightly negative relationship between the variables in girls. When permissiveness, which correlates −.46 in the study, is considered along with punitiveness, a stronger relationship appears. Low permissiveness and low punishment were associated with medium aggression, as was high permissiveness and low punishment; high permissiveness and high punishment were associated with high aggression.

In a study supportive of the above, Bandura and Walters (1959) correlated the relationship between antisocial behavior and parental control. Mothers of aggressive boys were found to be significantly more permissive than mothers of the control group. Both mothers and fathers of aggressive boys were found to be significantly more punitive of aggression toward other adults than the control group, but there was no appreciable difference for punishment of aggression toward siblings or peers.

The influence of modeling behavior has also been shown in a correlational study (Bandura, 1960). He found that families whose fathers displayed indirect or direct hostility toward their wives had sons who tended to display generally more aggressive behavior. Similarly, mothers who showed indirect hostility and who responded aggressively when instigated had sons who were relatively high in aggression.

The correlational studies thus tend to generate more support for the frustration-aggression hypothesis than do the experimental studies. However, even in these cases the support is not overwhelming. Clearly there remain a number of problems in the study of the frustration-aggression hypothesis.

The major problem explicated at the beginning of this section indicated that agreed upon definitions of the concepts of frustration and aggression were not available. It should now be more apparent that definitions are necessary for an understanding and interpretation of experimental and correlational results. In the experimental studies, aggression was at times conceived as deliverance of electrical shock to another organism, which fit Buss's restricted definition as well as that of Dollard et al. Aggression was also considered as the punching on inanimate bobo dolls or the striking of mallets, which does not fit Buss's definition. Similarly, frustration was operationalized in various ways: as verbal attack, punishment of aggressive behavior, and inability to complete a task. The multiplicity of operationalizations make it almost impossible to draw any consistent conclusions from the literature studied. The correlational studies clearly produced more support for the hypothesis, but one cannot be sure when the proper blocking by the frustrating instigator has occurred or how much frustration is necessary. The proper time in the behavior sequence clearly must be found. The fact that most of the experimental studies, regardless of the operationalization of the variables, do not lend support to the hypothesis leads us to conclude that more needs to be done than to correctly operationalize the variables in the proposed relationship. Political scientists need to be more careful when extracting hypotheses from other disciplines. As Lee Seechrest (1971) has stated: "It is amazing how many people in political science, sociology and anthropology have taken on the frustration-aggression hypothesis for their own use without realizing its still shaky status in psychology."

Studies which employ the frustration-aggression hypothesis may be deficient for a number of other reasons, including the "political" implications in the choice of this model. The hypothesis assumes that the problem of political violence concerns the alleviation of frustration experienced by those at the bottom of the political hierarchy. Men rebel because they are frustrated and hence angry (Davies, 1969; Gurr, 1970; Feierabend, 1966). They commit acts of aggression because they see no other means of changing either the system or their own situations. But it should be clear that the most consistent and destructive employers of aggression and violence are those who are in charge of the state. Do we interpret their actions as instrumental strategic responses or as the results of frustration when their system of order is being challenged?

Attitudes of aggression studies researchers have paralleled those involved in the study of conflict. Aggression has been seen as something to be resolved rather than managed. It has also been argued, however, that aggression is a major means of man's adaptation to the environment and necessary for his survival.

> The evolutionary approach proceeds from the thesis that aggressiveness in man (including the propensity to violence) is a product of evolution and can be understood only in terms of its functional contribution (at least as a behavioral category) to the ongoing survival problem of the species. Aggressiveness has aided man (and many other species as well) in adapting to the environment, that is, in goal directed efforts to satisfy his continuing survival needs and in coping with various stressful and threatening situations (both natural and man made) [Corning, 1971: 349].

An evolutionary adaptive approach considers violence as destructive aggression and argues that it is an attempt, albeit maladaptive, to cope with tensions in the environment. Although one may envisage certain situations where violence may be thought an acceptable alternative, or even the best alternative from a rational assessment of a situation, the approach rejects this choice as untenable for the survival of the species. Aggression is consequently treated as a subcategory of a number of different behaviors: "exploration, problem-solving activities, interpersonal competition, responses to stress or deprivation, and, of course, calculated instrumental violence" (Corning, 1971: 349).

Important questions still remain unanswered: what situations of problem-solving activities and attempts to cope with the environment tend to result in violence? What structural situations are likely to result in the need for violence as a problem solving activity, and how do these structures affect the survival chances of societies as collectives? To answer these questions we turn, in the next chapter, to quantitative studies of the impact of external factors on internal violence, and, in Chapter 4, discuss some structural conditions that result in the choice of violence as a political tool.

Chapter 3

THEORY AND METHOD IN STUDIES OF THE RELATIONSHIP BETWEEN FOREIGN AND DOMESTIC VIOLENCE

The last chapter indicated that violence in the domestic system affects, and is affected by, events in the environment. Social scientists have created analytically distinct subfields in their pursuit of political violence theory. One of the most familiar distinctions is that between the study of political processes within and between states, between comparative and international studies. The area of overlap in these two systems has been identified as the study of linkage politics (Rosenau, 1967; 1969). The study of linkages attempts to identify and assess those areas where two or more analytical systems overlap as well as the relationships that are produced. Thus, linkages are defined as "any recurrent sequence of behavior that originates in one system and is reacted to in another" (Rosenau, 1969).[1]

A number of earlier studies have been interested in linkages between foreign and domestic violence. Due to the differences in their conceptual approaches and methodological analyses these studies have produced contrasting results. However, they do share a number of conceptual problems and common results, despite their differences.

They have all employed a model which maintains a distinction between conflict management within and among nations. The dominant view is that the state is a conflict manager within the territorially bounded nation state, but merely a member of the "Hobbesian state of nature" in the international realm.

The use of physical force has been regarded by many writers as a characteristic feature of the political structure. Following Weber, we may identify the state as "that human community, which, within a given territory ('territory' is one of its characteristics) claims for itself (successfully) the legitimate monopoly of physical violence" (Gerth and Mills, 1958: 78). Government is thereby identified with legitimate use of force. It therefore becomes natural to dismiss governmental violence because it is viewed as normal. Research on violence within societies has concentrated on "abnormal violence" or what is commonly referred to as civil strife (Gurr, 1970).

Nardin has incisively discussed the sources of this conceptual problem. It is worth summarizing his arguments exposing the problems of studying linkages among the artificial systems which researchers construct to analyze "internal" and "external" behavior of nations. This involves the identification of the state as either a conflict manager, as Marx conceived the Hegelian conceptualization, or the state as a party to the conflict. In the vulgarized Hegelian conception:

> Conflict becomes the clash of special interests which it is the function of governments to resolve, and violence a form of partisan action which it is the government's task to manage with force, if necessary [Nardin, 1971: 14].

Marx, however, contends that: "Government, far from being above the special interests in society, in actuality constitutes a weapon employed by the dominant interests of the ruling class" (Nardin, 1971: 14). In the latter conceptual scheme the state's use of force is seen as the violence of a partisan faction, not as conflict management. This alternative construct advocated by Nardin approaches conflict management with the intention of

> reducing the violence of conflict between groups, including conflicts between political authorities and other members of the community or between rival authorities whether within national societies or in the international system [Nardin, 1971: 14].

Adoption of this approach, which accepts the state as party to conflict behavior, makes it easier to bridge the boundaries between the study of conflict within and between nations by proceeding with similar conceptual frameworks in both systems.

A second problem, which may have its sources in the first, is that these studies have dealt with conflict behavior in general without differentiating between violent and nonviolent behaviors. That is, they compounded the error of dealing solely with "partisan" violence with that of considering any collective conflict behavior, whether or not any actual physical violence took place. Thus, strikes, demonstrations, and protests, which have no violence associated with their immediate occurrences, are generally pooled with similar events which do result in violence, whatever the cause and whoever the initiator. It might be argued that it is an empirical question whether this lumping of violent behavior with other conflict behavior distorts the results. Nevertheless, the answer cannot be ascertained unless we distinguish between violent and nonviolent behavior and compare the results.

A third problem is the recent tendency for this type of research to be of a synchronic nature (dealing with phenomena that take place with many units but within the same time period), rather than diachronic (dealing with phenomena that take place over many time periods but within a limited space region). While for some research subjects the approach may not be crucial, attempts to determine the impact of events in one system on those in another should be concerned with interactions and processes of change over time. The first three studies to be discussed are exceptions, but their level of generality detracts from the usefulness of their results. With these three general problems in mind we will briefly look at a number of other studies to see what past research has yielded, in the hope that we can build on these studies and indicate more fruitful lines of inquiry.

Sorokin (1937) cites an earlier longitudinal study by Lee (1931) which found that internal violence in China clustered before, during, and after external wars. Sorokin carried out a massive longitudinal analysis of the ancient empires of Greece, Rome, Byzantium, and a number of European nations over fourteen centuries (525-1927). Unfortunately, in 1937, modern computer facilities were not available and the results were arrived at by "eye-balling" differences in the curves of internal and external disturbances. Sorokin reported that although there seemed to be a slight indication that internal disturbances tend to occur more frequently during and around years of war, upon closer examination the two processes tend to be independent of one another. Sorokin's analysis was based on time intervals of quarter centuries and centuries and thus does not yield very discriminant results, but rather explores gross trends for major outbreaks of internal and external violence. He states: "so far as century periods are concerned each process has led a course independent of the other without positive or negative association" (Sorokin, 1937: 488). Unfortunately, little use has been made of this data base since the adoption of computer methodology in the social sciences.

Raymond Cattell, in a number of attempts aimed at the discovery of culture pattern profiles, performed factor analyses on a number of variables representating national characteristics from 1837-1937. The first two studies (Cattell, 1949; Cattell, 1950), used sixty-nine nations and yielded twelve orthogonally rotated factors. The first two factors contain the variables of interest to the present study. As can be seen in Table 3.1, the internal and external dimensions appear to be independent of one another except for the inclusion of secret treaties on the size dimension (with a relatively low loading). In a third study, (Cattell, 1951) twenty-nine nations, whose data coverage had been considered poor, were dropped from the analysis. The forty nations that were left were chiefly comprised of the "modern industrial nations." This analysis (Table 3.2) yielded quite different findings. By limiting the sample population, Cattell found that the two processes were not as independent as the previous studies had shown, but rather both tended to load highly on the same dimension.

Table 3.1: Cattell et al. (1951): Cultural Pattern Profiles (1949, 1950)

Factor I Size

.65 many political assassinations
.52 many riots and local rebellions
.33 frequency of secret treaties

Factor II Cultural Pressure vs. Direct Ergic Expression

.63 high frequency of clashes with other countries
.62 high frequency of participation in wars
.60 high frequency of treaties with other countries

Table 3.2: Cattell: Cultural Pattern Profiles (1952)

Factor III Cultural Pressure and Complexity vs. Direct Ergic Expression

.70 large number of clashes with other countries
.66 large number of riots
.60 large number of treaties contracted
.60 large number of secret treaties contracted
.58 frequent involvement in war

A series of studies, which also utilized factor analysis and, in addition, multiple regression techniques, were initiated by R. J. Rummel in the Dimensionality of Nations Project. All subsequent research in the linkage between internal and external behavior of nations has relied heavily on the DON project for either methodology and/or data base. The relationship between domestic and foreign conflict behavior in these studies was based on an analysis of twenty-two variables for all nations with populations over 800,000 in the years studied. For the Rummel data (1955-1957) the sample was 77 nations, while the Tanter data (1958-1960), as a result of population growth and the inclusion of newly independent nations, included a universe of 83.

The Rummel studies utilized three separate steps in analyzing the data. First, a factor analysis was performed on all twenty-two conflict variables together to see if foreign and domestic conflict variables loaded on the same factors. Second, a factor analysis was done on each of the foreign and domestic conflict variables separately to determine if there were different dimensions of foreign and domestic conflict. Third, the foreign and domestic dimensions discovered in the second step were regressed upon one another to determine the strength and direction of the relationships.

The first Rummel (1963) and Tanter (1964) studies found a slightly positive association between domestic conflict behavior and the more belligerent forms of foreign conflict behavior, although for the most part, the independence of the two were reconfirmed (Tables 3.3 and 3.4). Subsequently, the 1955-1957 data were annually reanalyzed by Chadwick and, with a one year time lag, this independence was further supported. Tanter (1966) lagged the 1958-1960 data on the 1955-1957 data and found that there was a slight increase in the relationship. He suggested that: "There may be no simple relationship between domestic and foreign conflict behavior, but there may be a causal relationship which is being obscured by other phenomena" (Tanter, 1966: 60). The studies also identified separate independent dimensions within both the internal and external dimensions themselves. Rummel (1963: 67) states:

> The domestic conflict behavior of nations varies along three uncorrelated dimensions: turmoil, revolutionary, and subversive. The foreign

Table 3.3: Rummel: Predictions of Domestic Conflict Behavior*
Independent Variables War, Diplomacy and Belligerency

Dependent Variables	Standard Error	Multiple R	Prop Var. R^2
Turmoil	2.31	.37	.14
Revolution	1.70	.27	.07
Subversion	1.01	.14	.02

*n = 77 (Rummel:1963:20)

Table 3.4: Tanter: Predictions of Domestic Conflict Behavior*
Independent Variables War, Protests, and Severance of Diplomatic Relations

Dependent Variables	Standard Error	Multiple R	Prop Var. R^2
Anti-Government Demonstrations	.35	.32	.10
Revolutions	.27	.20	.04

*n = 83 (Tanter:1964:54)

conflict behavior of nations varies along three uncorrelated dimensions: war, diplomatic, and belligerent.

Tanter (1964) found that the revolutionary and subversive dimensions were subsumed under one internal war dimension, while the turmoil dimension and the foreign conflict behavior dimensions compared favorably to the Rummel study.

The early DON project data base did not include the majority of African nations, since they were not independent in 1955. Collins (1969), employing the same general research strategy put forth by Rummel and his successors, investigated the relationship between foreign conflict behavior and domestic disorder in Africa in the period 1963-1965. In this study, the first to investigate the relationship within one "region," Collins reports that there were differences between his results and the preceding work.

> Foreign violence is related to conditions of domestic disorder more so in African states than elsewhere, although the size of the correlations indicates that foreign violence is a product of other factors as well, which have not been tapped in the present research [Collins, 1969: 36].

However, there was no support for the hypothesis that official military hostility and violence was a product of domestic disorder in the preceding year. Nor was there any evidence found for a causal link between the severity of foreign conflict and any patterns of domestic disorder. The importance of the study lay in its finding that "region" as a variable might influence the pattern of the relationship between foreign and domestic conflict.

Jonathan Wilkenfeld (1968; 1969) attempted a reevaluation of the Rummel and Tanter data in "an effort to both retain and properly identify any relationships which had previously been obscured" due to the methods used to analyze the data. Consequently he rearranged the nations into groups according to type of nation, to see if type of nations has any bearing on the exhibited relationships. The nations were divided into three groups (factor names assigned by Banks and Gregg, 1965) centrist, personalist, and polyarchic. A correlation analysis (simple Pearson product moment) was performed for all possible pairs of domestic conflict dimensions and all foreign conflict dimensions (see Rummel, 1963) for the 1955-1960 data in the first study, and for all possible pairs of conflict behavior found independently by Wilkenfeld in the second study with time lags of one and two years. (Data found in the Rummel, 1963 and Tanter, 1964 studies.)

A weakness in the first Wilkenfeld design was the use of factors which (1) did not correspond to those found in the 1958-1960 data source (see Tanter, 1964) and (2) are based on factors obtained previous to the division of the sample into different types. In the second design Wilkenfeld (1969) corrected the first mistake and obtained factor analyses which corresponded to the entire data set, but did not correct the second (dividing the sample into groups before deriving new factors). Thus he assumed equivalence across isolated groups primarily to discover if there existed within group differences in the relationships among these variables. This, I would suggest, is an error of method which distorts the results (see Stohl, 1971 results).

The analysis did have some interesting results, however. There was no particular relationship between any pair of internal and external conflict dimensions which held for all three groups. Wilkenfeld posited the type of nation and the nature of conflict as the determining factors in the relationship between internal and external conflict. In a third study Wilkenfeld and Zinnes (1973) employed Markov analysis to determine if foreign conflict behavior affects the changes or transitions over time between levels of domestic conflict behavior. Once again the Rummel and Tanter data were utilized and the factor scores were the data for the Markov analysis. When all nations were analyzed "the foreign conflict behavior 'war' as measured by the variables most highly loading on this factor (military actions, wars, mobilizations and foreign killed) affects transitions in domestic conflict behavior as captured by the turmoil factor (strikes, riots, demonstrations) primarily when domestic conflict behavior is at a very high level" (Wilkenfeld and Zinnes, 1973: 335). When the nations were analyzed by nation type it was again found that foreign conflict behavior primarily affects transitions in domestic conflict for the personalist and polyarchic states.

Stohl (1971) reanalyzed the Rummel (1963) data after dividing the nations into groups by political type corresponding once again to the Banks and Gregg study. Supporting Wilkenfeld's conclusion, political type of nation was found to play an important role in determining the conflict patterns within and between nations. The factor analysis of the measures of conflict behavior found that there were different patterns of domestic and foreign conflict behavior for each of the political types. Further exploration of the relationship, through multiple regression analysis with a one year time lag, revealed moderately strong relationships in polyarchies, between diplomatic exchanges and general internal strife (r = .54), and between war and internal crises (r = .45). In the personalist nations increases in foreign conflict behavior were associated with small increases in domestic conflict behavior (multiple R's — .25, .45, .33, .40); while in the centrist cluster, there was no relationship discovered. It was hypothesized that the two major factors differentiating the three groups, level of social control and decision latitude, could account for the differences. As degree of social control and decision latitude decreases, elites are faced with greater pressure to justify their foreign conflict behavior to their populations. It was suggested that higher information levels and inadequate elite justifications of behavior may help to explain the higher association between foreign and domestic conflict behavior found in polyarchies and personalist nations (Table 3.5).

Table 3.5: Stohl (1971): Predictions of Domestic Conflict Behavior Independent Variables: Foreign Conflict Behavior Dimensions

Dependent Variables	Standard Error	Multiple R	Prop Var. R^2
Centrist			
Demonstration	.73	.17	.02
Subversion	.60	.15	.02
Revolutionary	.68	.27	.07
Personalist			
Spontaneous	.69	.25	.06
Subversive	.71	.45	.20
Revolution	.71	.33	.10
Individual	.75	.40	.16
Polyarchic			
General Internal	.44	.57	.32
Crises	.74	.48	.23
Guerilla Wars	.77	.46	.21

Two more recently reported studies of the relationship have attempted a more sophisticated analysis through the use of canonical analysis. Canonical analysis attempts to maximize the linear correlation between sets of variables. Phillips (1970), in a study of the impact of the conflict environment of nations via a regression analysis of the residuals in the canonical analysis of the DON data for 1963, found evidence for a relationship between internal and external violence. He states (Phillips, 1970: 37):

> The conclusion here is that nations displaying domestic violence, having a low percentage of population in agriculture, who have tended to experience unlawful changes of offices in the recent past, and have a high cost of living index, tend to send more military violence to the environment than would be expected, given normal exchange with the environment. In other words, modernizing nations experiencing inflation and internal violence possibly associated with unlawful change of leadership, are likely to respond militarily to their environment.

It should be noted that these types of states more closely resemble the personalist type differentiated by Wilkenfeld and Stohl and the African states studied by Collins, lending support to those findings.

The most ambitious use of the Rummel and Tanter data to date has been the attempt by Hazlewood (1973) to adapt this data for use within a general systems model. Hazlewood's main hypothesis tested concerning this chapter's interest was that "to the extent that internal variety is more extensive than internal constraint, the system stresses are likely to be manifested in foreign conflict behavior at a later time period" (Hazlewood, 1973: 162). Employing the Tanter and Rummel foreign conflict behavior factors and subsequent canonical and path analysis Hazlewood found that:

> Existing internal variety (societal diversity and turmoil), even without extreme economic expansion to activate it, is strongly associated with external conflict behavior. Economic stability, societal heterogeneity, and internal turmoil predict best to war [Hazlewood, 1973: 169].

However, the path analysis revealed that, "The strongest path in the model relates turmoil to war for 1958-1960 through prior warfare" (Hazlewood, 1973: 183). This would indicate that past foreign conflict behavior is more important than domestic conflict in predicting war.

What conclusions can we draw from this series of studies? Rummel (1963), Tanter (1964), and Sorokin (1937) suggest that foreign conflict behavior is generally unrelated to domestic conflict behavior. Reanalysis of the Rummel and Tanter data sets have been undertaken, however, and evidence for a relationship between foreign and domestic conflict has been found in a number of studies. Wilkenfeld and Zinnes (1973) and Hazlewood (1973) have found that foreign conflict behavior is related to domestic conflict behavior of low severity. Wilkenfeld (1968; 1969), Wilkenfeld and Zinnes (1973), Stohl (1971), Phillips (1970), Collins (1969), and Cattell (1951) have found that foreign conflict behavior is related to domestic conflict behavior in certain nation types or regions.

Perhaps the most important finding is that, despite the almost complete disregard for external interactions in theories of domestic political violence, there has been increasing evidence for the existence of a relationship between internal and external violence. This relationship has been found consistently in nations which have been characterized as personalist and polyarchic, with the strongest relationships occurring in polyarchic nations.

In the following chapter the political system of the United States, a polyarchic modern industrial nation, will be discussed with reference to the sources and dimensions of conflict that are likely to occur and the effect of war on these dimensions of conflict.

NOTE

1. Linkages could be considered as links between a nation and the international system (as in Rosenau [1964] "Internal War as an International Event), between a nation's domestic structure and foreign policy (as in Kissinger "Domestic Structure and Foreign Policy" in Rosenau [1969]), or between a nation's internal and external behavior on any number of economic, social, or political dimensions (see Rosenau, 1969 for many of these possibilities).

Chapter 4

THE POLITICAL SYSTEM: Stratification and Patterns of Conflict and Violence

Introduction

In this chapter we present two interrelated arguments which provide a framework within which we can develop and test hypotheses concerning the impact of war on the pattern of conflict and violence in the United States. First, we introduce the concept of stratification and demonstrate how it relates to the political system. Second, we discuss the specific ways in which war affects conflicts and violence between the different strata in American society.

A major assumption of this chapter is that the political system distributes values within the social system. The term values, as defined by Lasswell (1958), refers to desired goods and conditions. A second conception of value, which hereafter is referred to as value criteria, refers to the ideological principles that guide social organizations and systems. The structures of the system consist of the component parts' tendencies to interact in certain ways and the constraints that specify or limit these alternative interactions (Buckley, 1967: 128).

The development of a political system and corresponding structures which distribute societal values implies a choice as to what is valued by members of the political system and as to the basis on which values should be distributed. In political systems characterized by conflicts of interest, conditions in social relationships in which individuals or groups hold incompatible or mutually exclusive value criteria, politics is the distribution of values by authorities. Weber (1947: 154) termed the structures developed to perform these functions political "in so far as the enforcement of its order is carried out continually within a given territorial area by the application and threat of physical force on the part of the administrative staff." Either individuals or groups who do not receive the rewards they want will voluntarily comply with authoritative decisions, or the regime will attempt to force them to comply.

Stratification

Deciding what to value implies inequalities among values and value criteria and a system of ranking values in order of their distribution importance. Parsons (1953: 97) suggests that stratification is the process by which individuals and groups are ranked in a social system on the basis of a "common" value criteria. Thus, there may be natural differences among individuals of age, sex, or race, but clearly there is some structure(s) in the social system that translates these differences into social inequalities. The position taken here is that a society's stratification system, enforced by the political structures, accords individuals places in various categories or groups. These categories determine the distribution of valued goods and conditions to the individuals in those categories. Some social structures may usefully be seen as segmented. A segmented system has attribute groups whose members are readily identified by a number of established criteria. "Segmented society, therefore, is the polar opposite of individualistic society— a society characterized by the apparent interchangeability of all inhabitants" (Rogowski and Wasserspring, 1972: 37). To illustrate this notion, imagine a very simple stratification system where rank is accorded on the basis of race only, and within this social system there are only three races: black, white, and yellow. Let us further suppose that there are only three strata or ranks in the system (defined as analytic levels of stratification systems composed of one or more segments and/or individuals based on the combination of one or more value criteria): top, middle, and bottom. The whites occupy the top, blacks the middle, and yellow the bottom. In this white dominant society a black man is easily identified by his race and ranked in the place provided for his segment of the population—the middle strata. In order to change that rank (and hence the distribution of valued things), he would have to change his skin color, a process involving high psychic as well as social costs, or band together within his attribute group to collectively attempt to change the ranking system. This could occur in isolation from or in conjunction with the yellow segment. If this attempt were successful, the new dominant segment would include the black and/or yellow segment, and a black individual would move up in the ranking system and increase his relative share of valued things.

In essentially the same fashion the nation may be seen as a stratified social system. In adopting this approach, four working assumptions concerning behavior in status systems need to be explicated (see Rummel, 1971).

(1) Behavioral dimensions are linearly dependent on status.
(2) Segment behavior is directed toward higher ranking segments, and the higher a segment's rank the greater its status behavior, or in other words, the greater will be the segment's frequency of behavior involving status interactions.
(3) High rank segments support the current social system.
(4) Segments emphasize their dominant rank and others' subordinate ranks in interactions.

The first assumption is the key notion of status theory; status shapes behavior and can be specified by a linear relationship. In this case, linearity simply refers to a direct relationship between status and increases in nearly every type of social behavior.

This linearity is intuitively sensible and status theory provides no reason to assume otherwise. Status itself is a linear continuum running from low to high (most desirable) and the higher a status the more a particular behavior. And this linearity appears to be confirmed by empirical results [Rummel, 1971: 50].

If status is linear and desirable, then segments will desire to move toward the top of the status hierarchy. The closer segments move toward the top, the greater will be their interest in maintaining the system which accords them their status rewards. At the same time, since they have acquired higher status and system interaction is based on status, higher segments will emphasize their status positions in interactions with those below them in the status hierarchy. As Coser has said (quoted in Rummel, 1971: 53):

> To the vested interests, an attack against their position necessarily appears as an attack upon the social order. Those who derive privileges from a given system of allocation of status, wealth and power, will perceive an attack upon these perogatives as an attack against the system itself.

Within this framework it is possible to distinguish six types of conflict behavior in which the incompatibility of these values may be manifest:

(1) Reaction: Attempts to decrease the relative distribution of values to lower segments and increase the distribution of values to the dominant segments.

(2) Conservatism: Attempts to maintain the status quo in the face of changing conditions.

(3) Accommodation: Attempts to increase the size of the dominant strata through individual or segmental mobility.

(4) Reform: Attempts to increase the distribution of values to lower strata and decrease the distribution to dominant strata.

(5) Radicalism: Attempts to improve the relative ranking position of lower segments and thus the distribution of values.

(6) Revolution: Attempts to change the value system and the replacement of one value system with another.

It is not the purpose of this chapter to develop a detailed historical account of how and why certain stratification systems came into existence. However, we should digress somewhat and indicate how natural (age, sex, race) differences may become translated into social inequalities.

Davis and Moore (1949) suggest that stratification was functionally necessary for organized social existence. The argument they present, however, is circular. They suggest that: "As a functioning mechanism a society must somehow distribute its members in social positions and induce them to perform the duties of these positions" (Davis and Moore, 1949: 435). They assume that social positions in societies are unequal in their importance for societal survival, and that they vary in degree of ability needed for persons to fulfill these functional tasks. Thus, the positions are unequal. Therefore, societies must offer unequal rewards to induce persons to take demanding positions. Because they are unequal, "rewards and their distribution become a part of the social order and thus give rise to stratification" (Davis and Moore, 1949: 435).

This argument's weakness is inherent in most explanations using the functionalist framework. The explanation focuses from present to future events, or past to present events, and seeks to understand or explain present phenomena in terms of their consequences for the continuity, stability, or survival of the complex of which they are a part. What is functional for the system cannot be established by assuming that a system works on functional prerequisites and then gathering evidence that support this observation. The functional nature of a system must be translated into propositions that can be falsified by empirical tests.

It is also necessary to emphasize the distinction between unequal distribution of tasks and social inequality. There is no inherent reason to conclude that social inequality must follow from natural or distributive inequality. To do so confuses the distributive and relational aspects of inequality. Distributive aspects refer to the ways in which different factors such as occupation, skills, and power are distributed in the population while relational aspects refer to the ways in which individuals differentiated by these criteria are related to one another within a system of categories (Beteille, 1969: 13).

Theories of social stratification should deal with the relational rather than the distributive dimensions of natural inequalities, because stratification refers to the ranking of different individuals and groups in the social system, rather than the values and natural inequalities which distinguish them.

How do individual natural differences become translated into social inequalities? We have suggested that individuals or groups may move up or down stratification systems and have indicated the basic patterns of conflict that result from the interaction of the segments within the system. Three commonly identified dimensions of inequality are considered responsible for the movement of individuals and groups within the political system: class, status, and power—the economic, social, and political dimensions.

Class, Status and Power

We will follow Weber in distinguishing these three dimensions, beginning with class. In his terminology, we consider classes not as communities, but rather as possible bases of communal action.

> We may speak of a 'class' when (1) a number of people have in common a specific causal component of their life chances, in so far as (2) this component is represented exclusively by economic interests in the possession of goods and opportunities for income and (3) is represented under the conditions of the commodity of labor market [Gerth and Mills, 1958: 181].

These conditions of class rest on the basic dimension of the ownership of property. Property and lack of property are thus the basic categories. There are subsidiary dimensions which interact with this basic cleavage between the property owning group and the labor market. The credit, or money market, is the basis of conflict between debtors and creditors, and the commodity market is the basis for the conflict between buyers and sellers or landlords and tenants. An individual's class is determined by his shared location in the economic hierarchy which is based on his place in the process of production, distribution, and exchange. Class, for Weber, thus refers to individual's common life chances in the economic order. For Marx this was the explanation of stratification systems. Behavior could be predicted, he stressed, by knowledge of individual's class. Shared class consciousness was the cornerstone of political and social behavior. Since there were obvious instances in which class did not predict behavior, Weber was not satisfied with class as the explanation of social behavior and sought the causes of these divergences.

Weber stressed that social action could not be predicted from mere knowledge of economic classes. Class for Weber (and as it will be used here) does not include Marx's concept of shared consciousness. Weber felt that status groups hindered the carrying through of sheer market principles. The concept of status situation was meant to add to the use of the class and to reinterpret Marx's concept of false consciousness.

> In contrasts to the purely economically determined 'class situation' we wish to designate as 'status situation' every typical component of the life fate of men that is determined by a specific, positive or negative, social estimation of honor. This honor may be connected with any quality shared by a plurality and, of course, it can be bent to a class situation [Gerth and Mills, 1958: 186-187].

Status rests upon community estimates of social prestige accorded its members. Status lines may follow class lines, and this is more likely in periods of economic stagnation than in times of flux. Unlike the class situation, which can be determined by a knowledge of economic facts, status rests on the "mysterious" procedure of social evaluation. As a result, people may share similar class situations (according to the "objective" economic facts) yet assume vastly different positions in the status hierarchy. An extreme case would be the example of the unemployed, bankrupt aristocrat. A more familiar example is the case of the nouveau riche entrepreneur. Veblen's concept of conspicuous consumption describes the phenomena of people who achieve equal class strata in objective economic terms and attempt to spend money to demonstrate the need for others to accord them higher status rank. Weber summarizes this point when he states that:

> With some over-simplification, one might thus say that 'classes' are stratified according to their relations to the production and acquisition of goods, whereas status groups' are stratified according to the principles of their consumption of goods as represented by special styles of life [Gerth and Mills, 1958: 193].

Dahrendorf presents a quite different approach to the determination of class structure. He suggests that "In terms of our model, the term 'class' signifies conflict groups that are generated by the differential distribution of authority in imperatively coordinated associations" (1959: 204). The distribution of authority consequently becomes the cause of conflict group formation. He also asserts that because authority is dichotomous (your social position either has it or it does not), there are always two, and only two, conflict groups in associations (Dahrendorf, 1959: 172-173). Authority, in Dahrendorf's work, is employed in a specific sense and is differentiated from power by the concept of legitimacy. It must be understood within the context of its use which is only in what Dahrendorf refers to as imperatively coordinated associations. Thus, while power is tied to the individual, authority is always associated with social position.

This definition of class is considerably broader than either Marx's or Weber's and although precise, it probably blurs a number of important considerations in the relationship between class (as defined by Dahrendorf), status, and power. The usefulness of Weber's distinction is implicitly recognized when Dahrendorf later employs socioeconomic status as an intervening variable which helps explain the intensity and violence of class conflict. While his approach is broader than that of either Marx or Weber, Dahrendorf still needs to fall back on the distinctions made by Weber when discussing class conflict. These inconsistencies between class, status, and power may have violent consequences for the social system, but for the moment we will return to Weber and discuss these inconsistencies later in the chapter.

The third dimension of inequality, the political, is the allocator of power and the control center of the stratification system. For Marx, the economic system was the crucial determinant of inequality. Weber demonstrated that status could modify the economic system. He was also aware of the role this interaction had in the allocation of political power. Weber defined power as: "the chance of a man or a number of men to realize their own will in a communal action even against the resistance of others who are participating in the action" (Gerth and Mills, 1958: 180).

Within this framework the political dimension seems to be the crux of the stratification system. Those who dominate the political system by using the currency of power determine the relative importance of the various political parties (defined in the broadest sense as organized groups for action) and, thus, the relative importance of the various class and status distinctions. Position in the political order is determined by degree of societal power—in other words the ability to determine social action regardless of content. How, then, did one originally gain political power? Obviously, one's position in the political order was dependent on the economic and social power one possessed, one's ability to determine the allocation of goods and services, and one's ability to use prestige to "buy" action. There is, nevertheless, an obvious interdependence among the three dimensions. Weber never satisfactorily explains how the three aspects of power interrelate. Perhaps there is no general answer.

Marx, of course, claimed that the economic system was paramount. Within the economic dimension we know that the main determinant of power is the ownership of property. The type of property owned is itself an important power determinant. Under feudal systems land ownership was the crucial resource of political power. Land ownership meant the ability to mobilize the people who depended on the landlord. Power was possessed in proportion to the amount of land owned and the size of the population it directly supported. The industrial revolution, or the new epoch of capitalism, changed the currency of economic power. The property class which assumed dominance was comprised of the factory owners. The great industrial giants generated a greater ability to mobilize capital and increase wealth. The balance of power in society shifted from the land to the factories. There are, however, manipulators, individuals who hold vast political power but who are not ranked very high in terms of status or class. Weber used the example of the ward boss. A contemporary example is Mayor Richard Daley of Chicago who enjoys tremendous power through the political machine he has created.

While we agree with Weber that social action cannot be predicted by mere knowledge of economic class and struggle, we also agree with Marx that the economic system is the most important dimension in the allocation of political power and, thus, is the key to the stratification system of any society. The economic dimension provides the basic substructures for the stratification of American society. Kolko (1969: 6) stresses that "the essential primary fact of the American social system is that it is a capitalist society based on grossly inequitable distribution of wealth and income that has not been altered in any essential manner in this century." That the economic system is considered dominant should come as no surprise to anyone familiar with social structure in the United States. The ethic of achievement in America is based on money, and economic good is associated with social good. The cliché that what is good for General Motors is good for the country is repeated in various ways at all levels of society. Rogowski and Wasserspring (1972) have asserted that the highest segment is the one which produces the most social goods. In the case of capitalism, the segments at the top should be those who control the means of production. That would be the case if the stratification system were built from a tabula rasa, but the system has developed upon other systems. Although the controllers of the means of production are at the top, they share this pinnacle with those who were already there when the transition to capitalism began. Their positions were welded onto the existing inequitable distribution. The political power and social prestige held by those segments previously at the top allowed them to "buy" their way into the new stratification system.

It would be convenient for researchers if this were not the case. If pure economic variables determined the ranking system, or if there were only one ranking system with which researchers had to concern themselves, research would be much simpler. However, as should be clear by now, any attempt to rank an advanced industrial society and all its segments through the analysis of only one dimension is doomed from the start. A more realistic representation of rank must take into account economic, racial, ethnic, religious, educational, and governmental ranking systems. These subsystems overlap, interact with, reinforce, and cut across one another and, depending on the issue or situation, may have varying importance and strength.

To illustrate the interaction of the different ranking systems, we introduce the peculiar interplay between race, ethnicity, and class. Jackson and Curtis (1968: 125) have discussed this interplay as a methodological problem: what kinds of social phenomena are race and ethnicity?

Most studies have been based on one of two different answers to this question: race and ethnicity are treated as rank systems, or racial-ethnic groups are treated as nonstatus groups with some of the same characteristics and consequences as social classes. Considering the latter assumption first, racial-ethnic groups have always confused social class analysis because, like social classes, they consist of interacting groups (or at least loose networks of interaction and communication) and associated subcultures, and they often have opposed group interests. Nevertheless, these categories are regarded as vertically differentiated into classes and horizontally differentiated into racial and ethnic groups, so that a class structure exists within each group, and vice versa. . . . This alternative approach is that race and ethnicity act as rank systems, as values distributed in the population. Hence a Polish name would contribute to a low-status evaluation just as a low ranking occupation would.

Jackson and Curtis have thus illustrated the assumptions inherent in two alternative approaches to the treatment of race, ethnicity and class, when researchers attempt to construct ranking systems which combine all three concepts. One alternative would be applicable when the society in question did not exhibit any marked racial or ethnic prejudice and where racial and ethnic groups were found at all levels of society. The second alternative would apply in a society where prejudice was marked and individuals were limited by their race or ethnic group from moving freely through the stratification system despite their achievements. In the second society class conflict would be muted because of the more easily identifiable stigma of race or ethnicity.

It is highly significant that those societies that have very little class conflict exhibit a great deal of ethnic conflict. In the U.S.A. there is race conflict, in Ireland there is religious conflict, in Belgium it is language, in Sweden it is racialism—in fact these societies exhibit every conceivable type of social conflict except overt class conflict [Jenkins, 1969: 124].

Bottomore has also commented on the process whereby race and ethnicity have muted the influence of economic factors in determining class distinctions. Referring to the black population in the United States he asserts:

The existence of this large, relatively homogeneous, easily identifiable and exploited group, has meant that every white American, even the lowest paid laborer, possesses a certain social prestige which raises him, at least in his own view, above the level of a proletarian. Immigration has worked in the same way to raise the social position of the American workers [Bottomore, 1965: 45].

In an interesting paper, Norbert Wiley has attempted to show how the black movement can be interpreted as a special form of class conflict in the commodity market.

The concrete grievances of Negroes often center around the need for commodities, which they either cannot afford or are not permitted to buy or rent, and much of the non-violent action, such as sit-ins, has been an attempt to obtain forbidden commodities and to secure complete freedom with this market. When these actions have been most militant, as in the rioting and store looting of recent summers or the rent strikes in some urban slums, the economic side of the conflict has been squarely in the commodity markets. This is not to say that the major economic disabilities of Negroes are in the commodity market, even when this market is conceived broadly. Certainly unemployment, low wages and other labor market troubles are the Negroes most serious problems. But sometimes the response is incommensurate with the stimulus, because something mediates. The commodity market in the United States is the economic area most saturated with status and symbolic values, and the pure status conflict or "tribal" confrontation confrontation between Negroes and whites finds issues in the commodity market more easily than in other areas. Commodity protests define the interaction of status and class conflict in this case. This response, moreover, is in line with what might be expected from people with only a marginal allegiance to the working class and a predominantly 'lumpenproletariat' mentality [Wiley, 1969: 202].

Stratification and the Political System

We have stated that the dominant segments' ranking of the remaining segments determines the ranking system. Does this imply that there is a power elite (in C. Wright Mill's terms) that conspires to decide what the system will be? Pluralist democratic theorists would have us believe that the major organized interests in society, most notably capital and labor, compete on equal terms, and that no single group is able to achieve any permanence in positions of power. The groups thus continually compete with each other for the right to rule. E. E. Schattschneider has commented on the pluralist perspective: "the flaw of the pluralist heaven is that the heavenly chorus sings with a strong upper-class accent. ... The system is skewed, loaded and unbalanced in favor of a fraction of a minority" (Schattschneider, 1960: 31). It was this unbalanced, upper class accent of the American power structure that led C. Wright Mills to describe the power elite. There has been too much contrary evidence of mobility, and not enough of conspiracy within the upper stratas of society, to allow for a strict power elite interpretation. But the fact remains that there has been a continuous domination of a few segments of society over the rest.

E. Digby Baltzell was the first to systematically document the composition of the American social upper class and their backgrounds. From this study (Baltzell: 1958) it can be seen that the members of the social upper class and corresponding social register are rich businessmen and their descendants, although the register is unlikely to contain members of the ethnic rich such as Irish Catholics and Jews. However, there has been much movement within the middle strata and even the entry of some of the upper middle class into the top strata. But at the bottom, class is a very different phenomenon, "a pariah group that is collectively identified and denied social mobility either individually or as a class. It is an ascribed as well as an achievement criterion that maintains these groups at the bottom" (Jenkins, 1969: 130).

The important question is whether we can determine if certain identifiable segments are indeed in favored positions in the American social structures. A ruling elite model would imply that the same persons conspire to control a wide variety of issues. We posit, instead, a governing strata model which suggests that there are a number of segments which receive a disproportionate share of the country's income, own a disproportionate share of the country's wealth, and contribute a disproportionate number of its members to the controlling institutions and key decision making groups in the country (Domhoff, 1967). Below we distinguish four major ranking systems and their approximate order of prestige within rank, and suggest that there is a pattern to the holding of dominant positions in American society.

Racial	Ethnic	Economic	Religious
White	Northern European	Employer	Protestant
Black	Southern European	Landlords	Catholic
Oriental	Eastern European	Employees	Jewish
Indian	Latin	Farmers	
	African		
	Asian		

This suggests that white, Anglo-Saxon, Protestant employers hold positions in the dominant segments in society. With few exceptions, this has been the case. The majority of the exceptions have involved those landlords and large landholders in the South and West where manufacturing was not as important as in the East. In terms of people who hold offices of national power and control major U.S. corporations, there has been a predominance of families who reside in the northeastern United States and who are white, Protestant, and successful businessmen (Domhoff, 1967; Baltzell, 1858). For a graphic illustration of this phenomenon in one city the reader should consult Warner's "Yankee City" studies (Warner and Lunt, 1941: Table 7, 225).

The government reflects the dominant ranking of the segments in the important subsystems. The government itself may also be seen as a ranking system. At the top of this system is the U.S. Federal government. We know that there are often disputes between federal and state or local governments as the case of school integration illustrates. In the state of Mississippi, federal troops assisted James Meredith in enrolling at the University of Mississippi against the will of the Mississippi state government.

This implies, then, that the dominant segments, through their disproportionate share in the nation's wealth, prestige, and power, in large part determine the continuation of the segment ranking system and, hence, the resultant distribution of goods and services. This existing distribution of values in large part determines potential future contribution in both positive and negative terms. This determination of values provides the major basis for political conflict and violence.

The interactions involved in attempts to maintain or adapt the rank system to changes in the environment involve the systems concept of morphostasis and morphogenesis.

The former refers to those processes in complex systems environment exchanges that tend to preserve or maintain a system's given form, organization or state. Morphogenesis will refer to those processes which tend to elaborate or change a system's given form, structure or state. Homeostatic processes in organisms, and ritual in socio-cultural systems are examples of morphostasis, biological evolution, learning, and societal development are examples of morphogenesis [Buckley, 1967: 58-59].

In terms of the conflict patterns elaborated earlier, reaction, conservatism, and accommodation would be examples of morphostasis. Reform, radicalism, and resolution would be examples of morphogenesis, because they change the rank system of a society, or create a new system.

Changing economic conditions may cause the potential contributions of a segment and the distribution of goods among segments to rise or fall. This creates a rank disequilibrium, in Galtung's terms (1964), which increases the tension in the system to the point that the dominant groups have to adapt the system, increase the available goods, or put the lower strata in a position to attempt to alter the current distribution of goods and services, as well as the ranking system. It is interesting to note that while Galtung suggests that disequilibrium intensifies aggression, Dahrendorf asserts that, on the contrary, the greater the disparity between socioeconomic status and authority positions the less intense class conflict will be (Dahrendorf, 1959: 218).

War and the Pattern of Conflict and Violence

The American economic system, as a capitalist system, has within it the seeds of such problems. Marxists have not been the only observers who have recognized this dilemma. The major thrust of liberal economics has been to create the conditions under which the internal economic system would be maintained within the current system. The members of the American dominant segments have thus often seen international, as well as domestic, economic expansion as the key to domestic prosperity and social peace. Joseph Frankel (1964: 54) suggests that:

One of the most significant relationships within the environment is the interaction between domestic and foreign affairs. On the basis of the relative security and isolation from foreign affairs it has been customary for British and American thinkers and statesmen to believe that the two domains are separate and that domestic affairs prevail. Very different is the tradition of the continental countries where such separation has never taken place.

While we would not dispute the importance of this connection, we would disagree with Frankel's assertion that American statesmen believed that the two realms were separate. Many national leaders operate in both the domestic and international arenas. To stay in power they must solve problems in both realms. Domestic affairs prevail in the sense that international decisions are judged by their domestic consequences. William A. Williams (1970: 4), commenting on the period concerned in this study, has stated that American leaders

> were primarily concerned with obtaining markets for surplus manufactured goods and venture capital, and with acquiring access to cheap raw materials needed by the American industrial system. That industrial orientation became increasingly clear during the twentieth century as American leaders struggled to build and maintain an international system that would satisfy the interrelated economic, ideological, and security needs and desires of the United States as they defined those objectives.

During periods in which American leaders attempted expansion of the free marketplace, the United States became involved in a number of wars. Williams asserts that there were "wars to apply the principles; and wars to defend the freedom and the prosperity that the expansion of the principles had obstensibly produced for Americans" (Williams, 1970: 46). While this is not a necessary or sufficient explanation for all U.S. war involvement, for whatever reasons the U.S. became involved in war, the consequences of war for the stratification and political systems were significant.[1] In the following pages we discuss these consequences.

In subsequent chapters we will investigate periods (after 1890) when the United States was involved in war, to determine whether these periods are characterized by increasing violence as the lower segments of society clashed with higher segments over the distribution of scarce values. In the periods following successful war the dominant segments were strengthened both because of increased markets and their ability to provide more goods within the same ranking system. However, another result of the participation in war should be an increase in social dislocations (internal migration, upward mobility for semi-assimilated segments) which both intensify demands and threaten the positions of the dominant segments. Attainment of war objectives means the dominant segments will have increased goods to distribute, in addition to their increased status, and will attempt to protect the gains of war from those who seek to have the system adapted to provide a different distribution. Periods after successful war can be expected to show a continuation of domestic violence, with increases in the amount of violence between top and bottom and with more violence being directed downward from above.

> Every successful imperialist policy of coercing the outside normally—or at least at first—also strengthens the domestic 'prestige' and therewith the power and influence of those classes, status groups and parties under whose leadership the success has been attained [Gerth and Mills, 1958: 170].

In less successful wars, concluding with either empty victories or stalemates, the same pattern of social dislocation should be repeated, but dominant segments will not have increased prestige or increased goods to distribute. They will, however, once again wish to protect the political system that insures their dominance and will perceive internal challenges more in zero-sum terms than if they had gained expanded markets. Hence, violence directed against lower segments will again prevail. The lower segments will not receive benefits from the war, despite their intensified demands and will direct more violence toward dominant segments after less successful wars than after successful wars.

Plausible Rival Hypotheses

The discussion in Chapter 3 indicated that at least three quite contradictory hypotheses can be found in the literature dealing with linkages between internal and external conflict behavior.

(1) Increase in foreign conflict behavior are related to a decrease in domestic conflict behavior (Simmel, 1955; Coser, 1956; Wright, 1941).

(2) Increases in foreign conflict behavior are related to an increase in domestic conflict behavior (Wilkenfeld, 1968, 1969; Stohl, 1971; Collins, 1969).

(3) Foreign conflict behavior is generally unrelated to domestic conflict behavior (Rummel, 1963; Tanter, 1964).

Although Simmel (see Chapter 2) has suggested a somewhat contradictory set of hypotheses within his work, few researchers have attempted to deal with the problem. He suggests that conflict with outgroups leads to increased cohesion in the ingroup. Thus researchers looked for decreases in internal conflict behavior (Tanter, 1964; Stohl, 1971). He also suggests, however, that conflict with outgroups makes the group more intolerant of internal dissent, and that the group may also look for internal enemies who may be forcefully removed. This would suggest that while certain types of conflict may decrease, other forms of conflict may, in fact, increase. Previous research has not concentrated on violence done by and for the state, but rather has focused on violence against the "legitimate" authorities.

The following hypotheses concerning the ways in which war stimulates changes in the internal political system and resultant conflict and violence are postulated in this study.

Hypothesis 1: Wartime economic mobilization brings new groups into the productive process and enhances the economic positions of groups relative to the dominant segments, thus intensifying economic conflict and violence.

Hypothesis 2: Wartime social mobility increases the status positions of underdog social groups, relative to the dominant segments, which increases the hostilities between them.

Hypothesis 3: The economic and social changes of the war generate demands for the reallocation of political power and rewards which intensifies conflict and violence between top and bottom.

Corollary 3A: Success in war provides a greater number of goods to be distributed by dominant segments while increasing these segments' power and prestige. This intensifies their efforts to maintain the control of the political system while increasing their ability to do so. The result is an increase in violence directed downward by dominant segments which is greater than the increase of violence by lower segments.

Corollary 3B: Lack of success in war decreases the power and prestige of dominant segments and provides no additional goods to distribute. This intensifies their efforts to maintain control of the political system without increasing their ability to do so. The result is an increase in violence directed downward which is matched by an increase in violence directed upward by lower segments attempting to maintain the relative gains accrued to them during war.

In the following chapter, we will discuss the procedures employed to test the hypotheses generated herein, and the problems of translating information on violence during war periods into testable form.

NOTE

1. In causal modeling terms the difference between Williams assertion that the wars were caused by dominant leaders attempting to defend their positions at home and the position taken in this chapter, that there is an interactive effect between war and the stratification and political systems may be distinguished in the following figures, where A presents the logical consequences of Williams argument and B the position taken in this chapter.

Stratification system / Political system —+→ War —+→ intensified internal conflict and violence

Figure A

Stratification system / Political system ; War —x—+→ intensified internal conflict and violence

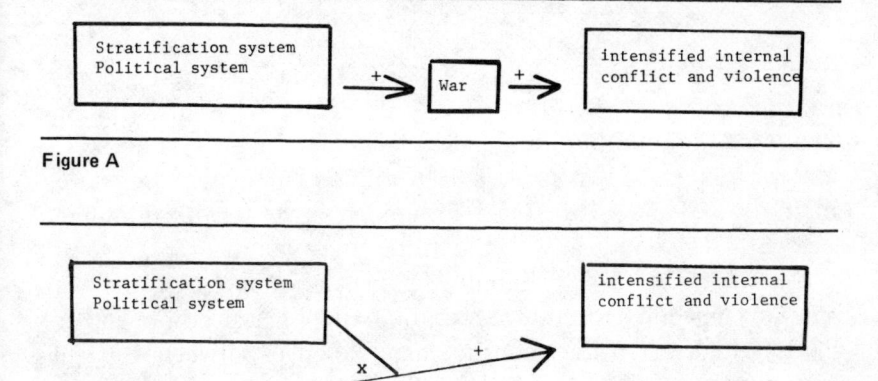

Figure B

Chapter 5

RESEARCH DESIGN AND THE CONSTRUCTION OF INDICATORS

Introduction

In the preceding three chapters we have criticized earlier efforts to explain the interaction between domestic and international political violence and have indicated a theoretical framework and a number of plausible hypotheses through which we posit that we may more profitably explore this linkage. In this chapter we detail the method by which we gather data, transform this raw material into meaningful variables and indicators, and test the usefulness of the hypotheses.

Any attempt to contribute to the development of a theory concerning the causes of violence within societies which is cognizant of the interaction between domestic and international violence must employ a research design that allows the basic interaction pattern to be tested. The criterion of testability, as stated previously (see Chapter 2) is its falsifiability. In other words, the hypotheses tested must be able to stand up to tests which in principle can disprove it. The research design we adopt must therefore be one which allows for the rejection of our conjectures.

In the following section, we will discuss the procedures employed to test the hypotheses generated herein, and the problems of translating into testable form information on violence during war periods.

The Interrupted Time Series Quasi-Experimental Design

In order to observe the impact of war on the type and extent of domestic political violence, we require a design that will allow for the introduction of the independent variable only at specified times in the sequence of events. The subject of study does not allow us to introduce the independent variable (United States participation in war) whenever we would want to provoke a change in the domestic violence measures, as we would be able to do within the confines of the laboratory experiment with individuals or small groups, or within the context of the program of a simulation. Rather, we must recreate the logic of a laboratory experiment utilizing naturally occurring phenomena.

The purpose of experimentation is generally to create the conditions under which the experimenter can separate the influence of confounding variables from those independent variables he is interested in pursuing and then to assess the relationships between these variables and his dependent observations. The researcher is interested in observing interpretable variation in an independent variable and detecting if the change in the independent variable has had an effect.

Campbell and Stanley (1963) have developed a number of designs that allow the researcher to artificially re-create experimental conditions. These quasi-experimental designs are appropriate when there is no ability to manipulate the independent variables or to randomize the treatment groups. In other words they are appropriate when the events are socially given. Thus as Caporaso (1973: 9) has noted,

> Quasi-experimental designs are rooted in conditions where there is no ability to manipulate the stimulus and no control through matching and randomization over competing stimuli. Experimental stimuli occur naturally, in a richly textured environment, with no active intervention of the researcher.

The researcher intervenes only in so far as he identifies, after the fact, an experimental input and indicates what that input is stimulating, through the careful development of theoretical hypotheses and observation. The particular quasi-experimental design which we will utilize in this work is the interrupted time series design. This design involved periodic measurements on the dependent variable(s) obtained at equally spaced time points (months in this case) and the introduction of the independent variable(s) or experimental input somewhere in the series. The design may be diagrammed as follows.

Interrupted Time Series Design

Pretest	Posttest	Pretest
$x_1, x_2, \ldots, x_m$	$x_{m+1}, x_{m+2}, \ldots x_n$	$x_{n+1}, x_{n+2}, \ldots$
Experiment (a)		Experiment (b)

Where "x" is any indicator, and where time is specified by 1,2, . . . ,n+k, and where experiments 'a' and 'b' are two different experiments. The first pretest series has 'm' data points, the second 'n,' etc.

The object of this design (as in all experimental designs) is to determine whether a change in the dependent variables(s) has occurred after the introduction of the experimental input. Explanations of what change has occurred and why can follow only after it has been established that a change in the dependent variable has indeed taken place. We are interested in two major questions (see Caporaso, 1973: 11):

(1) Did a nonrandom change occur in the vicinity of the experiment?
(2) Is the change attributable to the occurrence of the experimental input?

The determination of whether a nonrandom change has occurred in the dependent variables is the function of significance tests. These tests are used in conjunction with appropriate theoretical models which dictate where to look for discernible shifts in value.

Significance tests assess the difference between the expected and observed (or pretest and posttest expected in the case of the double mood test) value points or distributions of points during the months before and after the experimental input—war.

> Conceptually, then, in the interrupted time series analysis a 'true change' is one that changes the junction of the series, or one at least that is not interpretable in terms of the series' past function. Change will therefore occur under the following conditions: (1) When there is a discontinuous shift away from the trend line due to the impact of a substantive variable, (2) if there is a change in the rate of change (slope) or mean level of the variable (intercept) or (3) if there is an error exceeding the limits of the probability model [Caporaso, 1973: 25].

The tests used and their descriptions may be found in Appendix I. The identification of nonrandom changes, while crucial to experimentation, is only the first step in the process of establishing the credibility of hypotheses. It is also necessary, (1) to increase confidence by examining likely confounding sources of error in data sources and the procedures of collection and transformation, and (2) to distinguish plausibly rival substantive hypotheses. Next we indicate some likely trouble spots in both the data and the procedures employed to transform this data into indicators which test the hypotheses.

Data Collection and Construction of Indicators

There will be five quasi-experiments in this study, each at the time of United States participation in war. During the period of the study, the United States was involved in the Spanish-American War, World War I, World War II, the Korean war, and the Vietnam war. The dependent variables to be studied are the type and extent of domestic political violence.

Domestic political violence will here be defined as all collective non-governmental or governmental attacks on persons or property resulting in damage to them that occur within the boundaries of an autonomous political system. For operational purposes "collective" refers to twenty or more people. This will exclude most purely criminal acts and juvenile delinquency, and yet will encompass the majority of political violence. The phrase "within the boundaries" is meant to exclude events such as raiding across international boundaries and attacks mounted abroad by dissident exiles.

Sources

The primary source of the domestic violence data for this study was the *New York Times Index*. Where possible this primary source has been supplemented by information in the stories themselves. The coverage was also checked by comparing the events found in the index with a number of historical accounts and documentary studies for the period. The study is essentially an analysis of violence reported in the New York *Times* and an important issue is the adequacy of this particular source of information.

There have been many objections to and criticisms of work that has relied on the *Times* for information on conflict and violence in events analysis. Indeed, the most cursory examination of the newspaper will demonstrate that there are obvious biases in its coverage. This bias stems from two main concerns, first, differential concern for different regions and nations, and second, concern for the dramatic and unusual. As Gurr (1972: 56) points out:

> Wars, major natural disasters, coups d'etat, cabinet shakeups, and competitive national elections are among the kinds of events, mostly dramatic and violent, that seem reported with some consistency in mid-twentieth century newspapers. Lesser conflict events like demonstrations, clashes, and diplomatic protests are somewhat less likely to be reported, especially if they occur in countries that are not of great current interest. Minor outbreaks of conflict that might ordinarily be reported are sometimes overshadowed either by a very dramatic event or by the sheer number of similar events.

In line with this reasoning the use of the *Times* should not necessarily threaten the reliability of coverage for the United States. The *Times*, while it might be weak on coverage of certain areas of the globe, should always be concerned with dramatic violent events within the United States. The possibility that minor outbreaks of conflict might be overshadowed or missed because of the sheer number of world events indicates that the totals of violent events of limited magnitude and intensity are probably underreported and, hence, not included in the analysis. Nevertheless, a great number of these less violent events do, in fact, comprise the bulk of the data set.

Data Collection Procedures

The first step was to identify events by searching the *New York Times Index* for all the years included in the study and to record all information for all entries that appeared to indicate that a violent event had occurred. The coder then recorded all relevant information on the code sheets (see Appendix II). The month, day, and year were recorded as the date reported, except when the events were reported on the first of the month. These events were recorded as occurring on the last day of the previous month, because the data were later to be aggregated into monthly totals. Next, the coder had to determine whether the event was part of a larger event which was described in a number of articles. If so, the totals for the event were recorded as they would be for any single day event, except that the duration listed the appropriate number of days. If the type of event changed over a number of days (for example, if an event that began as a clash was followed by a clear attack by one of the conflicting groups against another the next day), the coder was instructed to code the series of daily violence as separate events.[1]

There are a number of problems for the researcher concerning the accuracy and reliability of counted and coded data. They are quite different from those confronted when dealing with handbook data or other statistical abstracts. The researcher in the data collection process must be cognizant of achieving an accurate picture of the phenomena being studied within the limitations of his data source, and must provide a check on the reliability of the procedures. These reliability tests are concerned with two main issues:

(1) whether the instructions are sufficiently detailed and explicit that anyone other than the person who devised them can use them; and

(2) whether the coder's biases or desire to obtain a particular result affected the coding of scoring of an index [Gurr, 1972: 58].

The simplest test for reliability of any type of context coding is the "percentage of agreement" between two coders or judges. A random sample of one hundred events were chosen and two assistants were given the coding instructions and asked to code the data. The percentage of agreement reached was .91 for the two assistants with the author and .89 between the two assistants.

Having recognized these problems, why then have we chosen to rely on the New York *Times?* Tilly (1969: 42), in his study of violent events in France, suggests that the newspapers provided the fullest enumeration of such events and their chief bias was toward the overreporting of events in large cities. This tendency to overreport violent events in large cities at the expense of small cities may be true of the *Times* coverage as well (it is obviously so in the case of overreporting events in New York City), but if we are aware of this, we can interpret the results with this bias in mind. In addition, in a recent study investigating the accuracy of the *Times* for this type of research, McCormick (1970) was unable to recommend anything of greater value.

Thus, while we are aware of the many objections made with respect to the use of the *Times* as a data source, we are also reasonably confident in the comprehensiveness of the coverage for the purposes of this particular study.[2] Multiple sources would obviously have been a corrective strategy for completeness, but given resource limitations, compromises had to be made. We have incorporated a second corrective, suggested by Gurr (1972: 56), involving reliance not merely on the sheer number of events but also on their magnitude and intensity. This procedure was incorporated in the construction of indicators of violence.

The data for the independent variable, war, were taken from the information provided in Singer and Small's *The Wages of War*. The independent variable in the quasi-experimental analysis is used merely as the interruption point around which pretest and posttest fluctuations in the dependent variable are measured. Because we are interested in the impact of the occurrence of war, we utilized the information providing the dates for the start and termination of war. Singer and Small's criteria (1972: 44-45) are the following:

Each war's opening data is that of the formal declaration, but only if it is followed immediately by sustained military combat. If hostilities precede the formal declaration, and continue in a sustained fashion up to and beyond that later data, the first day of combat is used. Even in the absence of a declaration, the sustained continuation of military incidents or battle, producing the requisite number of battle deaths, is treated as a war, with the first day of combat again used for computing duration.

Turning to *termination*, we again rely on a combination of legal and military events, with the latter more dominant. That is, the war's duration continues as long as there is sustained military action. If such combat comes to an end on the same day as an armistice is signed, and does not resume after the armistice, there is no problem. But if there is a delay between the cessation of military action and the armistice (which is very rare) or if the armistice fails to bring combat to an end, we then ascertain and use the day which most clearly demarcates the close of sustained military conflict. Similarly, the date of the peace treaty would not be used unless it coincided with the end of combat.

In the quasi-experimental analysis then, the interruptions were the months in which both the onset and termination of war occurred, as noted in the Singer and Small data set.

Variables and Indicator Construction

As indicated previously we are interested in both the type and extent of domestic political violence. We chose to divide types of violence between the two main dimensions.[3] The first differentiated political violence by the issue area which attempts to determine the issue or subject of conflict responsible for violent action. The determination of issue area was based on considering (see Chapter 4):

(1) the ranking system within which the violence occurred and where possible;
(2) the systemic target of the initiating group.

The ranking systems considered were the (1) racial, (2) ethnic, (3) religious, (4) educational, (5) economic, (6) political organizational, and (7) governmental. Events whose participants and

Research Design and the Construction of Indicators

targets were identifiable members of the ranking system were classified as such. Events whose participants and targets were identifiable members of the political organizational and governmental ranking systems were combined in a type of violence classified as political organizational. The events within each of the three types, social, economic, and political organizational were then aggregated by summing the monthly scores of the indicators of extent for each type of violence. The ranking systems follow the presentation in Chapter 4, and the systems and their contents may be found in the sample code sheet presented as Appendix II. Thus, in this first dimension of the type of violence, we differentiate among violence that occurred because of economic, social (racial, religious, ethnic, educational), or political organizational (foreign policy, ideological) conflicts that were not managed without recourse to violence.[4]

The second dimension of type of violence differentiates type by the perceived systemic intent of the initiating groups. The initiator of attack categories identify prosystem events (the initiating group seeks to maintain the status quo), antisystem events (the initiating group seeks to reform or challenge the status quo), and clashes where there are no clearly discernible initiators of violence in the event. In addition, the prosystem violence is subdivided into government initiated and dominant group initiated violent events during the period 1935-1970. The former is hereafter often referred to as repression and the latter as reaction. Both are considered manifestations of violent attempts at morphostasis, while antisystem violence is considered as an indication of morphogenesis.

The extent of violence refers to two dimensions, duration (number of total days of the event) and intensity (the cost of the event in terms of deaths or arrests). Property damage and injuries were to be included in intensity; however, the reporting was very irregular on these two variables and they were dropped from the analysis. As indicated above, the information for extent was collected for each event and then aggregated later by months for each of the types of violence. These monthly total scores were then used as the indicators of magnitude in the subsequent quasi-experimental analysis. The quasi-experimental analyses thus test the impact of United States participation in war by comparing pretest and posttest observations of magnitude and intensity for (1) economic, social, and political organizational violence and (2) antisystem, prosystem (both reaction and repression), and clashes. In addition, all violent events occurring within the period will be analyzed in order to obtain a composite view of the violence within any period.

These tests of the hypotheses consequently ignore much of the complexity of the environment within which the events take place. There are obviously a great number of other events and/or processes which occur coterminously with the independent variable, or which intervene between the occurrence of the independent variable and its presumed effects. The occurrences may therefore rival war as an explanation of the observed changes in the type and level of domestic political violence. The only correctives for this problem are good theory and comparison across cases. In this study the use of each of the different wars as cases allows for comparison across cases. If, given the great variance in internal and external conditions and change over time, the same patterns of relationships are discovered, idiosyncratic explanations of "cause" for the changes after each particular case will be less persuasive. In the following chapter we will present a description of the pattern of violent events within the United States, reporting the information collected for the study.

NOTES

1. It has been suggested that a reliability test ought to also have been performed at this stage of the two part coding process. While checks were made as to the thoroughness of the data set by comparing them with additional documents, no actual *test* of reliability was performed at this stage.

2. I am, however, not as confident as the editors of the index who suggest that if you cannot find it in the index perhaps it did not happen (Introduction, *New York Times Index*).

3. There are always problems with any attempt to categorize complex phenomena in a limited number of categories. In addition to the problems typical of any coding scheme, there are a number of conceptual problems concerning what is and what is not "political violence" that need to be mentioned. The following suggested examples of political violence were not included in this study:

(A) Are certain arrests for murder political? A political figure is convicted of murder (or for that matter any major "nonpolitical" crime). Is it a criminal or political act? Is the conviction concerned with political or criminal violence? Two familiar examples are the conviction and execution of Joe Hill for murder during the labor struggle at the beginning of this century, and the Connecticut trial of Bobby Seale for the murder of a Black Panther.

(B) Thomas Szasz suggests that the act of committing individuals to mental institutions is a political crime. In the United States, this criticism has been scoffed at by many. However, we do know that the Soviet Union has employed this means to rid itself of some of its most eloquent critics (Medvedev for one) and Szasz argues that this political crime occurs in the United States, though not perhaps at the specific order of the government.

(C) How does one classify the arrests of "political" individuals for drug possession? Is this "normal" law enforcement or a political arrest? Conversely is it political protest to smoke marijuana if more than twenty people are together. If they are caught together is it a political arrest?

(D) Studies of criminal law enforcement in the United States suggest that many of the arrests of blacks and other low ranked individuals occur in large part because of their blackness or low status. Moreover, in certain crimes such as rape the pattern has been that individuals are more likely to be arrested if the rape is of a white rather than a black woman, especially if the rapist is a black man. Should this be considered an area of political law enforcement, and if so, does rape sometimes become a political crime, as Eldridge Cleaver suggests?

4. An example of economic violence would be the violence arising from strikes or lockouts where laborers and management conflict. The clearest example of social violence is the race riot, but ethnic riots and religious clashes also comprise this category. Violent antiwar demonstrations or attacks by governmental authorities on political protestors would be a clear example of political organizational violence.

Chapter 6

AMERICAN VIOLENCE IN HISTORICAL PERSPECTIVE: Reaction, Repression and the Maintenance of the American Political System

Introduction

It was a dominant theme of Chapter 4 that conflict and violence arise from the inequitable distribution of values created by the American stratification system. Furthermore, we asserted that the central task of the political system is the protection and maintenance of this inequitable stratification system. Therefore, we argued that violence in America could most readily be identified as morphogenetic or morphostatic, violence aimed at either reforming and changing the system, or protecting it. In this chapter we will explore the validity and usefulness of this perspective by examining the magnitude and intensity of each of the types of domestic political violence previously identified (see Chapter 5) within the period 1890-1970. In Chapter 7 we will turn to the quasi-experimental analyses of the impact of war on these patterns.

We have discussed the criteria and procedures for the collection of information concerning violent events in the previous chapter.

Since data were collected primarily to examine the impact of war on domestic violence, some years within the period have been excluded. The data for the discussion have been analyzed for the following periods within which a war has occurred:

Spanish-American War	1890-1906
World War I	1913-1923
World War II	1935-1947
Korean war	1948-1956
Vietnam war	1960-1970

In addition, 1957-1959, the transition years between the Korean and Vietnam war periods, were also included. The discussion which follows provides information pertinent to the following questions concerning the above years:

(1) What is the distribution of American political violence by type, participants, and initiators?

(2) What is the magnitude and intensity for each type of political violence?

(3) What is the role of government agencies in violent events?

(4) What patterns of change in type, magnitude, and intensity of violence are evident with the passage of time?

The Distribution of American Political Violence

What is impressive to one who begins to learn about American violence is its extraordinary frequency, its sheer commonplaceness in our history, its persistence into very recent and contemporary times, and its rather abrupt contrast with our pretensions to singular national virtue [Hofstadter, 1970: 7].

Table 6.1 presents a composite view of the distribution of American political violence by type, magnitude and intensity. There were 2,861 recorded cases of domestic violence, but forty-four cases were excluded due to lack of information. The remaining 2,817 events resulted in 3,393 days of violence—18,985 arrests and 1,180

Table 6.1: Magnitude and Intensity by Type of Violence 1890-1970

	Soc.	Eco.	Pol.	Total
Number of Events				
Prosystem government initiated	172	65	221	458
Prosystem dominant segment initiated	229	2	10	241
Clashes	854	660	169	1,683
Antisystem	277	86	72	435
Totals	1,532	813	472	2,817
Duration				
Prosystem government initiated	192	69	238	499
Prosystem dominant segment initiated	238	2	10	250
Clashes	1,063	820	187	2,070
Antisystem	401	95	78	574
Totals	1,894	986	513	3,393
Deaths				
Prosystem government initiated	66	9	9	84
Prosystem dominant segment initiated	24	1	0	25
Clashes	648	267	34	949
Antisystem	69	42	11	122
Totals	807	319	54	1,180
Arrests				
Prosystem government initiated	1,325	524	3,627	5,476
Prosystem dominant segment initiated	117	0	0	117
Clashes	4,721	517	1,360	6,598
Antisystem	6,119	18	657	6,794
Totals	12,282	1,059	5,644	18,985

deaths. This measurement of violence is crudely mechanical and accounts neither for the qualitative nature of many events nor the relative political importance of different events. However, these findings do indicate that we have experienced much violence (over forty-five events per year, if distributed equally) and a substantial number of resulting deaths. The relatively low ratio of deaths per event (1:2.5) is consistent with the findings of Gurr

(1969: 552) who found that when compared to other Western industrial nations, the United States ranked first in the total magnitude of violence (duration, pervasiveness, and intensity) for the period 1961-1965 and twenty-fourth overall, yet ranked third in comparison with Western nations and fifty-third overall, in the intensity of violence.

The Initiation of Violent Events

We have classified violence according to the initiators of violent events in three categories: prosystem (subdivided into government initiated and dominant segment initiated), clashes (initiator not identified), and antisystem (subordinate segment initiated). Hofstadter (1970: 10) notes that:

> An arresting fact about American violence, one of the keys to the understanding of its history, is that very little of it has been insurrectionary. Most of our violence has taken the form of action by one group of citizens against another group rather than by citizens against the state.

Graham (1972: 203) concurs with this assessment and suggests that the American capitalistic system has made private institutions in America more important than American state institutions or than public institutions in other societies. Consequently violence has been most commonly directed by conflicting groups against one another rather than against the state. An examination of the events recorded as antisystem in this study is consistent with this assessment and indicates that the great majority of these events of violence by subordinate segments against both government and dominant segments focused on adapting particular features of the political system instead of replacing the system. These two factors, displacement of violence from the state to private groups and the limited nature of demands, may account for the discrepancy between the magnitude and intensity of violence. Perhaps there is a greater likelihood of intense violence when the institutions of the state are directly challenged and the state is the major target of reform initiatives. In general terms then, it appears that the greater the number of focal points for change, the greater the magnitude but the lesser the intensity of antisystem violence.

An examination of Tables 6.1 and 6.2 indicates that the majority of violent events were coded as clashes (59.8%). In these cases the reporting was unclear as to who first started the violence associated with these events. However, there were 699 clear initiations of violence by dominant groups and government agencies (24.8%), while 435 events (15.4%) were initiated by subordinate segments.

If American public institutions have not been the target of violence as often as expected, particularly in comparison to other nations, what has been the nature of government involvement in violent events? In Chapter 3 we indicated that most research on violence has concentrated on antisystem violence and clashes between authorities and subordinate groups and has excluded violence initiated by government agencies. We suggested that it was more useful to consider the state as a partisan faction rather than a neutral conflict manager. We should find, therefore, that the state intervenes and initiates violence against subordinate segments to a far greater extent than it becomes embroiled with dominant segments. Tables 6.4 and 6.5 provide overwhelming evidence for the rejection of the assumption that the state is a neutral conflict manager. Of the 1,083 events in this study in which government agencies' participation was recorded, only 56 (5%) brought these agencies into violent conflict with a dominant segment. Furthermore, when we examine the cases of the initiation of violence by government agencies, only 12 of 359 events were directed at dominant segments which were presumably exceeding the bounds considered proper to maintain the system.

In recent years it has become commonplace to discuss not only the ubiquity of American violence and the American ability to forget this history, but also the paradox that while the American past has been filled with violence, the United States has not suffered from chronic upheavals and continual political instability (see Hofstadter, 1970: 11 and Graham, 1972: 203). Tables 6.4 and 6.5 seen in conjunction with the following observations concerning violence in America should shed some light on this paradox.

Table 6.2: Initiators of Violence

	Number of Events		Percentage
Prosystem			
(a) by government	360		24.8
(b) by dominant segments	339	699	
Clashes	1,683		59.8
Antisystem	435		15.4
Total	2,817		100

Table 6.3: Participants in Violent Events

Segment	Number of Events Involved In
Federal	174
State	144
Local	811
White	981
Black	1,379
Indian	31
Oriental	7
Employer	489
Employee	4
Credit	20
Small Business	2
Employees	830
Unemployed	19
Northern European	15
Southern European	7
Eastern European	5
Latin	23
Asian	7
African	4
Republicans	8
Democrats	12
Right Wing	94
Left Wing	212
Antiwar	84
Women	19
Other political organizations	25
Protestant	4
Catholic	4
Jewish	36
University Administration	26
Faculty	1
Students	115
Missing data	133
Totals	5,722*

*2 segments recorded for each event, thus, there are 2,861 events recorded.

Table 6.4: Violent Events: Government Involvement and Conflicting Groups

Segment	Number of Events Involving Government Agencies
White	20
Black	408
Indian	17
Oriental	3
Employer	1
Credit	5
Farmer	1
Employee	226
Unemployed	14
Northern European	8
Southern European	2
Eastern European	3
Latin	13
Asian	4
African	1
Democrats	2
Right Wing	19
Left Wing	177
Antiwar	57
Women	18
Other	4
Jews	2
Students	78
Total	1,083

Gurr (1971b: 3) has identified two major sources of violence in America: defense of the status quo, which he contends is the most common private form, and reformist violence associated with subordinate groups advocating change. However, he notes (1971b: 5) that "the pattern which emerges when we look at reformist movements is that members are more often victims than attackers." Graham (1972: 208) concurs: "Much of our historic violence has served the dominant establishment—has usually been generated from the top of society and not the bottom—and has aimed at repression not innovation" (see also Hofstadter, 1970: 11).

While a majority of the violence reported in this study does not distinguish the initiator of the violent event, we can make four observations. First a much greater percentage of violence has been clearly initiated by both dominant segments and government agencies (to maintain political institutions protecting their posi-

Table 6.5
A. Government Agency-Initiated Violence by Subject of Violence

Segment	Social	Political Organizational	Economic	Total
White	2	0	0	2
Black	91	2	0	93
Employers	0	0	2	2
Employees	0	1	43	44
Unemployed	0	0	5	5
Northern European	0	8	0	8
Eastern European	0	1	1	2
Asian	0	3	0	3
Right Wing	0	8	0	8
Left Wing	0	134	7	141
Antiwar	0	18	0	18
Women	0	7	0	7
Jews	1	0	0	1
Students	2	23	0	25
Totals	96	205	96	359

B. Government Agencies: Initiation of Events by Subject

Agency	Social	Political Organizational	Economic	Total
Federal	1	59	5	65
State	12	10	6	27
Local	83	137	47	267
Totals	98	205	58	359

tions in the stratification system) than is initiated by subordinate segments against dominant institutions or groups. Second, we have evidence that many clashes were probably initiated by dominant rather than subordinate segments. Third, the government, when it does intervene in violent events, does so most often on behalf of dominant segments and against subordinate segments. Fourth, when the government initiates violent events, that violence is overwhelmingly directed at subordinate rather than dominant segments. If these observations are valid, the stability of American institutions appears to rest, in great part, on the willingness of dominant interests to use violent means to maintain these institutions. We will now turn to the examination of various types of violence classified according to subject of violence to see if our conclusions are consistent across subjects over time.

Social, Economic and Political Organizational Violence

SOCIAL VIOLENCE

Violent encounters in the American experience have most commonly been concerned with social issues (see Table 6.6), a category which is dominated by racial violence (95%). It is also the case that both the magnitude and intensity of racial violence is severely underrepresented in this study. There are two basic reasons for the exclusion of many events dealing with racial violence. The last sixteen years of the nineteenth century witnessed more than 2,500 lynchings of blacks and from 1900-1914 there were an additional 1,000 black victims (Link, 1967: 31). Many of these events were not reported at the time but rather were discovered through long years of searching through criminal records by the NAACP. Furthermore, many of the lynchings did not meet the operational requirements of this study of at least twenty participants. Nonetheless, they obviously represent a substantial magnitude and intensity of violence. While we have not included these events for quantitative analysis, an important point must be noted; the category of violence that is underrepresented is violence initiated by dominant segments against subordinates and this type of violence is rarely suppressed by government agencies.

The two primary forms of social violence are racial and nativist violence, the former referring primarily to blacks and the latter to ethnic violence. Two basic patterns of racial violence can be found

Table 6.6: Subject of Violent Events 1890-1970

	Subject	No. of Events	Percentage	Total Percentage
Social	racial	1,467	52.1	
	religious	35	1.2	
	ethnic	27	1.0	54.4
	educational	3	.1	
Economic	economic	813	28.9	28.9
Political	foreign policy	130	4.6	
Organizational	ideological	342	12.1	16.7
	Totals	2,817	100.0	100.0

Table 6.7: Magnitude and Intensity of Social Violence by Initiator

Initiator	No. of Events	Duration	Deaths	Arrests
Prosystem government initiated	172	192	66	1,325
Prosystem dominant segment initiated	229	238	24	117
Clashes	854	1,063	648	4,721
Antisystem	277	401	69	6,119
Totals	1,532	1,894	807	12,282

in the events in this time period. The last ten years of the nineteenth century and the first half of the twentieth were generally witness to interracial violence characterized by whites attacking blacks in urban race riots, or lynching them in the rural areas. Graham and Gurr suggest (1969: 373) that these "were essentially pogroms in which Negroes were victims of white aggression." Death and injuries were the direct result of fighting between blacks and whites. While this type of violence has not completely disappeared (white attacks of black civil rights marchers during the fifties and bombings during the sixties attest to this fact) it has been dominated in the sixties by a second form of violence. During World War II, large scale outbursts, contained primarily within the black community, began. The Detroit and Los Angeles riots of 1943 followed the pattern of earlier racial violence, but the Harlem riots of that year began the new pattern. The violence of the new pattern was directed mainly at property and other symbols of white authority and domination, and the deaths that resulted were primarily the result of the use of force by police and national guard units (see Janowitz, 1969: 393-422). With the exception of the past decade, the history of racial violence has been characterized by status quo segments attacking blacks.

Ethnic violence, commonly referred to as nativism, was mainly a phenomenon of the late nineteenth and early twentieth century. It characteristically involved white Anglo-Saxon Protestant attacks on recent immigrant groups who appeared to threaten their economic well being (see Higham, 1967). Private nativist violence appears to have been more ruthless than governmental violence. In 1895, for example, when the southern Colorado coal fields were involved in a long and violent strike, miners systematically massacred eighty-four Italian workers who were implicated in the death of an "American" saloonkeeper. However, when the threat of violence to ethnic America became too disruptive to the functioning of the political system—especially during wartime—the government interceded with questionably legal methods to deprive huge segments of the population of their most basic political rights. Two notorious examples of this technique are the government's campaign, during and after World War I, to deport aliens who currently or previously had belonged to left wing political organizations and the internment of Japanese-Americans during World War II. Earl Warren, later Chief Justice of the Supreme Court, then Attorney General of California, revealed the basic reasoning behind governmental policy when testifying before a congressional committtee to urge internment. He suggested that

> my own belief concerning vigilantism is that the people do not engage in vigilante activities so long as they believe that their government is taking care of their most serious problem [quoted in Brooks, 1969: 514].

The message was not lost on the Congress, and the Japanese-Americans were interned and denied their most fundamental rights, obstensibly in order to protect both themselves and the nation.

Violent collective conflict between ethnic groups and "native" Americans and/or government institutions has been a rare phenomenon since the end of World War I, when the rate of immigration was cut in half by a series of quota acts during the 1920s (Link, 1967: 330). This is reflected in the small number of events reported in this study. The pattern of social violence, with the exception of the past decade, has been one of dominant segment and government initiation of violent events.

ECONOMIC VIOLENCE

As indicated in Chapter 4, it is difficult to separate class, status, and power because of the obvious interconnections between the three determinants of stratification. Despite this difficulty, we have

Table 6.8: Magnitude and Intensity of Economic Violence by Initiator

Initiator	No. of Events	Duration	Deaths	Arrests
Prosystem government initiated	65	69	9	524
Prosystem dominant segment initiated	2	2	1	0
Clashes	660	820	267	517
Antisystem	86	95	42	18
Totals	813	986	319	1,059

attempted to distinguish violence that was primarily economic in origin by reserving this category primarily for labor-management related violent events. Taft and Ross (1969: 270-271), leading authorities on labor violence, have commented on its basic character.

> With few exceptions, labor violence in the United States arose in specific situations, usually during a labor dispute. The precipitating causes have been attempts by pickets and sympathizers to prevent a plant on strike from being reopened with strikebreakers or attempts of company guards, police or even National Guardsmen to prevent such interference.... Union violence was directed at limited objectives; the prevention of the entrance of strikebreakers or raw materials to a struck plant, or interference with finished products leaving the premises. While the number seriously injured and killed was high in some of the more serious encounters, labor violence rarely spilled over to other segments of the community.

The National Guard frequently was called out to suppress labor violence from the late nineteenth century to the time of World War II. This intervention in labor-management relations was rarely neutral, and for the most part, was aimed at protecting employers and the continuation of business as usual despite labor's demands. It is interesting to note that the Guard "was established first and most rapidly in the leading industrial states of the North that were highly vulnerable to labor unrest: Massachusetts, Connecticut, New York, Pennsylvania, Ohio, and Illinois" (Brown, 1969: 57). The National Guard system was complete throughout the nation by 1892 and after its contingents were no longer frequently utilized against labor, they were employed in racial and student violence.

The years of the most pervasive economic violence occur in the period from 1890-1940, during which time labor was attempting to obtain the right to organize and bargain collectively. Since the start of the Second World War economic violence has declined. This decline in violence coincides with the accommodation of union leaders and their unions as junior partners (management remained the senior partner) in the political system. For the most part, labor initiated violence had not been revolutionary, but has aimed at achieving acceptance of its ability to bargain collectively for wages, safety, and security. The transition from violent to nonviolent labor management relations occurred with the passage of the Wagner Act and the onset of World War II. The transition might have occurred twenty years earlier, if the government had not rescinded its requirement to accept union negotiation during the war, and had not reinstituted its policy of sending troops to trouble spots as a precautionary measure. Thus, 1937 rather than 1919 became the last year in which strikes involved the clash of armed forces or large scale assaults leading to heavy casualties. From 1937 on violent strikes exhibit little regularity and assaults on strikers by private company guards virtually disappeared.

Economic violence arose in most cases as a result of specific demands, and generally these could be met by a single employer or group of employers. Violence was therefore mainly private in origin and focus, but once again, when government agencies did intervene in violent events, they primarily did so on behalf of the dominant interests. It was not until the government intervened and legalized employees rights (withdrawing employers' ability to attack strikers with a cloak of legality) and minimized its direct physical intervention in strikes, that the violence of economic conflict was reduced.

POLITICAL ORGANIZATIONAL VIOLENCE

The major sources of political organizational violence in America have arisen out of government and dominant segment attempts to suppress "left wing" political groups and protest, and out of subsequent reaction to protest concerning foreign policy in general

Table 6.9: Magnitude and Intensity of Political Organizational Violence by Initiator

Initiator	No. of Events	Duration	Deaths	Arrests
Prosystem government initiated	221	238	9	3,627
Prosystem dominant segment initiated	10	10	0	0
Clashes	169	187	4	1,360
Antisystem	72	78	11	657
Totals	472	513	54	5,644

and U.S. war participation in particular. Table 6.3 identifies 212 instances of "left wing" involvement in violent events; the government has initiated 141 of these events and intervened in an additional thirty-six (see Table 6.5). The primary source of the remaining forty-five events were attempts by dominant segment organizational to attack "communists," anarchists, and other left wing groups.

The Palmer Raids of January 1920 are the most notorious example of government repression in action. Some four thousand persons were arrested in raids on the Communist party headquarters in thirty-three American cities. Eventually 556 alien members of the party were deported. These raids followed on the heels of the first Red Scare and were a logical culmination of the hysteria engendered by attempts to return a war weary nation to "normalcy." In 1917 Congress passed the Espionage Act which provided imprisonment of up to twenty years for persons who willfully made false reports to aid the enemy or obstructed the operation of the military draft. In a section dealing with the United States mail, the Postmaster General was empowered to deny the use of the mails to any matter which, in his opinion, advocated treason, insurrection, or forcible resistance to the laws of the United States. Link (1967: 210) asserts that "in effect the Espionage Act became a tool to stamp out dissent and radical but never conservative criticism" (see also Chafee, 1941: 51). This act was followed by the Sedition Act of 1918 which forbade disloyal, profane, scurrilous, or abrasive remarks about the form of government, flag, or uniform of the United States, or any language intended to obstruct the war effort. As a result of these two acts, 2,168 persons were prosecuted, 1,055 of whom were convicted, although only sixty-five had actually uttered threats against the president and ten had attempted sabotage. The legal groundwork for future Red Scares had thus been laid, and in the current climate of political opinion, was upheld by the Supreme Court by the "clear and present danger" doctrine enunciated by Holmes. It is notable that despite agreement on the limited threat that left or right wing political groups have ever posed to the political institutions of the United States there is such a disparity in both government agencies' preoccupation with these groups and the disparity in number of events involving the government and left wing organizations compared to right wing groups (see Table 6.5).

The second major source of political organizational violence concerns violence arising out of United States participation in war. While often referred to as antiwar violence, examination of the five wars in this study indicates that this is most certainly a misnomer. It is often the case that violence is associated with antiwar protests, but the initiation of violence is distinctly prowar in origin. The only war period in which there was no domestic violence directly associated with the war is that of the Spanish-American War. There were no major protests concerning the war and the only significant opposition to it concerned the acquisition of territory once the actual fighting had been concluded.

World War I established the pattern repeated, with target modification, in subsequent war efforts. Peterson and Fite (1957), in their comprehensive review of the war's opposition, identify only two instances from a long and appalling list of incidents in which the initiative for violence appeared to originate with the antiwar movement. In these two cases the antiwar groups initiated the events while prowar groups actually initiated the violence (see Brooks, 1969: 510-511). The war and patriotism became covers for the destruction of radical groups. The IWW which opposed the war, was virtually destroyed during it. "Mass jailings, beatings, and deportation of 'wobblies' took place in Arizona, Montana, and other states" (Brooks, 1969: 512). The Sedition Act, following on the heels of this direct action, suppressed dissent for the remainder of the war.

The attack on Pearl Harbor effectively eliminated the opposition to active war participation which had characterized the previous few years. However, as we have indicated, the government was fearful enough of reaction against Japanese-Americans to employ the dubious legal arguments to intern them. The inference is that the government did not want a repeat of the appalling events of World War I.

Brooks (1969: 514) suggests that the Korean war appears to be an excellent example of consensus through crackdown. Like the War of 1812, the Korean war generated one brief flash of opposition. This opposition took the form of a rally in New York City which was quickly and violently dispersed by police. The war had begun during a period of great peacetime repression and as a result, there was both little vocal dissent and little need for would-be vigilantes to aid the war effort.

The initiation of large scale commitments and fighting by American soldiers in Vietnam was accompanied by large antiwar protests. From 1965 through October of 1967 the pattern of previous war violence was sustained, and peaceful demonstrators were attacked by prowar groups and the police. After the Stop-the-Draft Week of October 1967, however, antiwar groups and students began to take the offensive. Unlike the police and prowar groups, the students and other antiwar activists attacked property, not people. The great majority of antiwar activity, however, remained nonviolent. The threat of violence from antiwar groups was now more forcefully prevented, as the events of Chicago and Kent State bear witness. But the break with the normal patterns of "antiwar protest" had occurred. For the first time youth and students were not only significantly in opposition, they and other members of dissenting groups initiated some of the violence that surrounded the protest concerning the war. The history of antiwar violence closely resembles the pattern of racial violence. Subordinate segments, after enduring attacks for most of the century, eventually began initiating violence themselves. This has happened consistently only in the past decade.

Conclusion

Finally one is impressed that most American violence—and this illuminates its relationship to state power—has been initiated with a "conservative" bias. It has been unleashed against abolitionists, Catholics, radicals, workers and labor organizers, Negroes, Orientals and other ethnic or ideological minorities, and has been used obstensibly to protect the American, the Southern, the White Protestant or simply the established middle class way of life and morals. A high proportion of our violent action has thus come from the top dogs or the middle dogs [Hofstadter, 1970: 11].

As Hofstadter suggests, we have discovered a persistent pattern of American violence, a pattern that is concerned with the utilization of violence for maintenance of the American political system. However, while we have been able to identify a larger proportion of violence that is explicitly pro- rather than antisystem, especially before the 1960s the largest category for each of the types of violence has been that of clashes. We have argued that many of these clashes appear, from the historical commentaries, to have been initiated by dominant segments and government agencies, rather than subordinate segments. There appears to be a consistent conservative bias to our data source as well as to the nature of violence. In the following chapter we will examine through the use of quasi-experimental analysis the impact that war has on this pattern of violence.

Chapter 7

THE IMPACT OF WAR ON DOMESTIC POLITICAL VIOLENCE

Introduction

In preceding chapters we have developed a number of hypotheses concerning the impact of war on domestic violence and then detailed a research design which evaluates these hypotheses. In Chapter 6 a descriptive account of the basic patterns of violence in America was presented which serves as background for the following analysis. In the first section of this chapter the results from the interrupted time series quasi-experiments will be detailed for each of the five war periods, and the five war periods will then be compared. In the second section we will evaluate the hypotheses explicated in Chapter 4.

The working hypothesis of the quasi-experimental design is that each of the "events" provides a socially given behavior that could be interpreted in the quasi-experimental terms of the design. The introduction of war is the event to be assessed. There is nothing else "in" the event other than the interruption point. The problem of interest is that of determining the degree of discontinuity

Table 7.1: Spanish-American War

	Slope Pre	Slope Post	Intercept Pre	Intercept Post	Single-Mood	Walker-Lev Test 1	Walker-Lev Test 3	Double-Mood
START (m = 99; n = 105)								
Duration								
All events	.01	−.01	1.95	5.23	.88	1.71	.85	.86
Clashes	.01	−.01	1.73	5.38	.92	2.57	.84	.84
Political	.00	.00	.11	.11	.21	.06	.18	.43
Economic	.01	−.01	.91	3.83	.53	1.11	2.52	1.53**
Social	.01	.00	.90	1.29	.86	1.07	.88	.99
Deaths								
All events	.03	.00	.15	3.34	.71	.58	.00	.02
Clashes	.03	−.01	.15	4.08	.71	.88	.00	.01
Political	None recorded after 29th month							
Economic	.02	.00	−.48	.69	.38	1.19	.16	.45
Social	.01	−.01	.37	2.66	.80	.23	.04	.16
Arrests								
All events	−.02	.00	1.81	.33	.10	2.14	.70	.91
Clashes	−.01	.00	1.22	.21	.07	1.24	.47	.74
Political	None recorded after 23rd month							
Economic	−.02	.00	1.26	.33	.07	1.20	.58	.82
Social	None recorded							
END (m = 104; n = 100)								
Duration								
All events	.01	−.02	2.19	7.18	.49	2.39	3.21	1.85*
Clashes	.01	−.03	1.98	7.15	.51	3.38**	3.09	1.83*
Political	.00	.00	.12	.17	.17	.02	.74	.85
Economic	.00	−.02	1.00	5.11	.11	1.91	4.81*	2.24*
Social	.00	−.01	1.03	1.80	.74	.88	.04	.16
Deaths								
All events	.02	−.01	.34	4.47	.66	.62	.05	.25
Clashes	.01	−.02	.34	5.25	.66	.93	.06	.27
Political	None recorded after 29th month							
Economic	.01	−.00	−.37	1.10	.34	1.09	.02	.09
Social	.01	−.01	.46	3.38	.76	.28	.09	.32
Arrests								
All events	−.02	.00	1.78	.61	.11	1.68	1.24	1.07
Clashes	−.01	.00	1.19	.44	.08	.96	.85	.89
Political	None recorded after 23rd month							
Economic	−.01	.00	1.23	.61	.08	.89	1.02	.98
Social	None recorded							
DELETED (m = 99; n = 100)								
Duration								
All events	.01	−.02	1.95	6.72	.60	2.99	1.83	1.33**
Clashes	.01	−.02	1.83	6.71	.58	3.57	2.15	1.44**
Political	−.00	−.00	.11	.17	.21	.00	.45	.67
Economic	.01	−.02	.91	5.02	.17	2.25	4.04*	2.00*
Social	.01	−.01	.90	1.77	.86	1.75	.35	.61

*Significant at the .05 level
**Significant at the .10 level

around the interruption point—the war. If the level of domestic violence was influenced by the event, it is hypothesized that the impact may be assessed by evaluating the differences (if any) between the pretest and posttest slopes and intercepts. The influence on the type of violence may be assessed by comparing changes in the levels of the different types. The war (event) was introduced and assessed for impact on the domestic violence series at the beginning and end of the war. In addition, the war months were deleted and the prewar and postwar months were directly compared.[1]

Quasi-Experimental Results

THE SPANISH-AMERICAN WAR

On April 4, 1898 the United States declared war against Spain. The impact of United States participation and its aftermath was evaluated for twenty-nine indicators (results Table 7.1).[2] There are only four variables which are significant at the .05 level, and an additional three are significant at the .10 level. At the start of the war interruption only the duration of economic violence shows a significant (.10) change. The intercept of these variables increases from 1 to 4 days per month.[3] The duration of violent clashes and "all events" intercepts, while not statistically significant, increase from 2 to 5.3 days per month with no appreciable slope changes. The number of deaths for violent clashes and all events also increase in the postwar months, but deaths related to economic violence do not. The third measure of intensity, arrests, shows no measurable slope or intercept changes.

At the end of the war the duration of economic violence (.05), clashes (.05), and all events (.05) all show increases in intercept level significant at the .05 level, with slopes remaining constant. Deaths, while again not statistically significant, increase for both violent clashes and all events; in addition, socially related deaths increase in the postwar period, with slopes remaining constant. This indicates a step level increase in violence. Arrests remain at a constant low level throughout the period.

It is expected that by deleting the war months the results should follow the pattern of the beginning and end of war interruptions.

Table 7.2: World War I

	Slope Pre	Slope Post	Intercept Pre	Intercept Post	Single-Mood	Walker-Lev Test 1	Walker-Lev Test 3	Double-Mood
START (m = 51; n = 21)								
Duration								
All events	−.14	.04	6.63	5.26	.92	6.28*	6.04*	3.25*
Prosystem	−.02	−.02	1.05	3.36	2.22*	.04	17.77*	3.98*
Clashes	−.11	.05	5.34	1.74	.49	7.49*	2.12	2.39*
Antisystem	.00	.01	.24	.30	.66	.16	.40	.73
Political	.00	−.04	.21	5.14	3.00*	3.06	28.01*	4.32*
Economic	−.14	.06	6.03	−1.54	.31	11.45*	.00	1.24
Social	−.01	.02	.40	1.23	1.64*	.73	4.19*	2.22*
Deaths								
All events	−.07	.07	2.64	−2.02	.76	1.79	.05	.70
Prosystem	.00	.00	.00	.15	I	.00	1.04	.92
Clashes	−.06	.07	2.43	−2.67	.76	1.86	.00	.53
Antisystem	−.04	.00	.21	.55	.02	.02	.30	.55
Political	.00	−.01	.00	.98	R	1.50	9.30*	2.39*
Economic	−.06	.04	2.26	−2.55	.36	3.22**	.19	.25
Social	−.01	.03	.38	−.75	.09	.26	.04	.37
Arrests								
All events	−.43	−.53	15.77	78.49	4.10*	.04	13.74*	3.36*
Prosystem	−.23	−.46	8.77	66.25	6.57*	.20	10.34*	2.82*
Clashes	−.19	−.04	7.00	8.58	.25	.86	2.18	1.71*
Antisystem	.00	−.03	.00	3.72	I	.12	1.00	.80
Political	.00	−.36	.07	55.41	177.19*	.64	8.31*	2.39*
Economic	−.43	−.16	15.70	19.79	.44	2.13	6.43*	2.90*
Social	.00	.03	.00	−.31	R	.06	.04	.28
END (m = 71; n = 61)								
Duration								
All events	−.04	−.09	4.74	19.69	.05	.93	24.11*	4.99*
Prosystem	.01	−.06	.53	7.56	.10	15.74*	14.16*	4.45*
Clashes	−.04	−.02	3.98	9.65	.00	.13	13.91*	3.64*
Antisystem	.00	−.02	.24	2.76	.61	1.59	7.48*	2.88*
Political	.03	−.06	−.34	7.47	.00	22.47*	1.84	2.07*
Economic	−.09	−.01	5.05	6.00	.43	2.44	13.72*	3.49*
Social	.02	−.02	.01	4.62	.74	1.61	7.18*	2.83*
Deaths								
All events	−.03	.01	1.87	4.90	.12	.16	3.02**	1.67*
Prosystem	.00	.00	−.04	−.15	.46	.00	.97	.98
Clashes	−.03	.03	1.73	2.05	.15	.42	2.04	1.33**
Antisystem	.00	−.02	.19	3.00	.09	.62	2.02	1.51**
Political	.01	−.01	−.11	1.18	.67	9.18*	.05	.57
Economic	−.03	.05	1.72	−2.87	.32	2.48	.58	.55
Social	.00	−.02	.26	4.65	.08	.03	1.65	1.29**
Arrests								
All events	.40	−.77	−.09	104.93	.63	6.61*	.81	1.25
Prosystem	.43	−.60	−4.01	81.59	.65	5.63*	.19	.74
Clashes	−.03	−.06	3.92	10.36	.13	.05	.62	.80

*Significant at the .05 level
**Significant at the .10 level

Table 7.2: World War I (Continued)

	Slope		Intercept		Single-Mood	Walker-Lev		Double-Mood
	Pre	Post	Pre	Post		Test 1	Test 3	
Arrests (Continued)								
Antisystem	.06	−.11	.00	13.13	1	2.50	2.65	1.83*
Political	.45	−.52	−8.18	72.90	.71	5.83*	.20	.76
Economic	−.05	−.11	8.11	14.01	.20	.15	.03	.23
Social	.00	−.02	−.02	5.16	.27	.06	.79	.91
DELETED (m = 51; n = 61)								
Duration								
All events	−.14	−.08	6.63	16.63	1.20	.56	27.41*	5.28*
Prosystem	−.02	−.05	1.05	6.12	1.17	2.25	32.15*	5.37*
Clashes	.11	−.02	5.34	8.50	1.11	2.14	13.05*	3.82*
Antisystem	.00	−.01	.23	2.23	.66	.64	6.05*	2.29*
Political	.00	−.05	.21	6.19	3.00*	6.11*	22.77*	4.40*
Economic	−.14	−.00	6.03	5.06	.31	3.85*	5.75*	2.72*
Social	−.01	.01	.41	4.12	3.32*	.03	13.91*	3.63*

*Significant at the .05 level
**Significant at the .10 level

While slopes remain constant in the prewar and postwar periods, the intercepts rise for duration of all events (.10) and violent clashes (.10) by almost five days per month, and for economic events (.05) by almost four days per month. There is, in conclusion, a step level increase following the initiation of war and in the postwar months. Duration of events is the most affected indicator, although the same pattern is exhibited by deaths. Violence related to economics appears to account for the duration increase, but apparently not for the increase in deaths.

WORLD WAR I

The impact of World War I was evaluated for forty-nine indicators (results Table 7.2). Thirty-two of these variables showed significant changes at the .05 level, and an additional four at the .10 level. The United States entered World War I as an official combatant in April 1917. At that time the number of days per month during which violence took place shows significant drops in level for all categories of violence, with the exceptions of political and prosystem initiated violence, which had sharp increases, and antisystem initiated violence, which evidenced no slope or intercept differences. There were a number of statistically significant slope changes, but the magnitude of those changes was very small for the variables showing significant intercept differences. Recorded deaths, with the exception of an increase (.05) from zero to one for political deaths, remained constant. The number of arrests in this period rose appreciably, with only the social and antisystem categories showing no change. Prosystem initiated and political arrests, as well as arrests in the all events category, showed an intercept increase of over fifty-five per month. In addition, there were four significant slope differences (all events, prosystem initiated, economic, and political). It is significant that while the number of violent events decreased in these months, political and prosystem initiated duration and arrests rose markedly after the involvement in war.

The end of the war in November, 1918, after nineteen months of official American participation, evidenced significant (.05) rises of duration in all categories of violent events. Significant slope changes also occurred in every category. Recorded deaths rose for all but prosystem initiated and economic events, with only politically related deaths evidencing any slope change, and that change was negative. The most marked change occurred in the recorded arrests category with significantly (.05) increased intercepts from less than 1 to 105 in the all events category. Antisystem initiated, prosystem initiated, and political events sharply increased, accounting for most of the change, but violent clashes and economic and social arrests, while not statistically significant, also increased. The end of the war thus brought clear step level increases in all categories of violence recorded, with prosystem initiated and political events demonstrating the greatest changes.

Once again the war months were deleted to compared prewar and postwar months for changes in the duration of violence. The seven categories tested (duration for all events, prosystem initiated, violent clashes, antisystem initiated, political organizational, economic, and social) displayed significant (.05) increases in intercept and, unlike the Spanish-American War events, significant negative slope changes as well. The exceptions were economic and social events, although none of the slope changes was of any appreciable magnitude.

WORLD WAR II

The impact of World War II was evaluated for a set of fifty-nine indicators (results Table 7.3). Nineteen of these indicators showed significant changes at the .05 level and an additional fourteen at the .10 level. The United States entered the war as an official combatant in December, 1941. The number of days per month during which violence took place shows significant drops in level at that time for all events (.05), prosystem (.05), social (.05), and economic violence (.10). Violence associated with clashes, on the contrary, evidences a significant (.05) increase. There were two significant slope changes; these occurred for prosystem (.05) and economic (.10) violence, but the actual magnitude of these changes was very small. Recorded deaths showed significant (.05), but slight, increases for all events, clashes, and social violence, and a significant but small decrease in economic related deaths (.10). Once again the magnitude of slope changes was very small, and only prosystem (.05) and economic (.10) deaths demonstrate significant changes. The number of arrests in this period rose significantly (.05) and appreciably for all events, prosystem and political violence. The remaining variables, while all evidenced decreases rather than increases, were not significant. Only arrests stemming from political violence demonstrated a significant (.10) slope change.

The end of the war in August, 1945, after forty-five months of American participation, evidenced significant (.10) intercept changes of duration in only two categories of violent events, prosystem and economic. There were no significant slope changes at this time. Prosystem (.05) and economic (.10) deaths showed the only significant changes in loss of life attributable to domestic violence. Once again, there were no significant slope changes. The number of arrests show significant intercept decreases accompanied by slope increases for all events (.10) and prosystem (.05), and a decrease in political (.05) arrests accompanied by a slight decrease in slope. It is significant that there were no recorded antisystem arrests after the end of the war.

The war months were deleted to compare the prewar and postwar periods. The duration of all events, prosystem, and social violence showed the only significant (.05) changes in intercept,

Table 7.3: World War II

	Slope Pre	Slope Post	Intercept Pre	Intercept Post	Single-Mood	Walker-Lev Test 1	Walker-Lev Test 3	Double-Mood
START (m = 83; n = 73)								
Duration								
All events	−.04	−.02	4.09	3.78	.18	1.84	5.44*	2.18*
Prosystem	−.01	.00	1.26	.52	.17	4.63*	3.57**	1.66*
Clashes	−.03	−.02	2.70	3.16	.10	.36	3.23**	1.72*
Antisystem	−.00	.00	.13	.09	.13	.10	.02	.12
Political	−.00	.00	.48	.24	.32	.72	.18	.33
Economic	−.02	−.00	−.00	.30	.12	3.78**	.00	.24
Social	−.02	−.02	−.02	3.22	.05	.01	8.19*	2.85*
Deaths								
All events	−.03	−.02	2.30	2.95	.25	.71	6.21*	2.38*
Prosystem	−.01	.00	.94	.15	.27	6.92*	3.32**	1.56**
Clashes	−.02	.02	1.37	2.79	.16	.01	3.93*	1.95*
Antisystem	.00	.00	.00	.01	I	.00	.25	.49
Political	.00	−.00	.02	.17	.12	.29	.43	.71
Economic	−.02	−.00	1.36	.26	.02	3.82**	1.85	1.15
Social	−.01	−.02	.89	2.52	.20	.05	3.81**	1.96*
Arrests								
All events	−.05	−.08	4.95	14.14	.05	.10	4.43*	2.12*
Prosystem	.00	−.08	.86	13.82	.18	1.29	4.50*	2.24*
Clashes	−.05	−.00	4.09	.32	.06	1.99	.23	.33
Antisystem	None recorded							
Political	.00	−.01	.33	14.09	.22	3.30**	6.89*	2.83
Economic	−.03	−.00	3.07	.41	.07	.67	.02	.22
Social	−.02	.02	1.20	−.36	.07	.54	.47	.60
END (m = 128; n = 28)								
Duration								
All events	−.02	.02	3.26	−.98	.01	.28	.59	.11
Prosystem	−.00	.04	.95	−4.50	.50	3.09**	1.27	.55
Clashes	−.01	−.02	2.20	3.54	.21	.02	.18	.38
Antisystem	−.00	.00	.11	.00	.10	.01	.08	.28
Political	−.00	.01	.41	−1.74	.39	1.23	.74	.73
Economic	−.02	.01	2.10	1.39	.23	.08	2.96**	.94
Social	.00	.01	.65	−.64	.04	.02	.10	.33
Deaths								
All events	−.01	−.03	1.52	5.18	.12	.15	.13	.54
Prosystem	−.01	−.01	.69	1.69	.15	.05	4.50*	1.58**
Clashes	−.00	−.02	.84	3.49	.16	.11	.04	.12
Antisystem	.00	.00	−.01	.00	.32	.03	2.16	.85
Political	.00	.00	−.01	.00	.33	.02	2.15	.88
Economic	−.01	−.02	1.02	2.80	.22	.06	2.65	1.27**
Social	.00	−.01	.49	2.39	.25	.09	.14	.03
Arrests								
All events	.02	.24	2.46	−32.41	.49	.77	1.74	1.53**
Prosystem	.06	.24	−.91	−32.41	.67	.72	4.12*	1.99*
Clashes	−.03	.00	3.37	.00	.16	.08	.92	.43

*Significant at the .05 level
**Significant at the .10 level

Table 7.3: World War II (Continued)

	Slope Pre	Slope Post	Intercept Pre	Intercept Post	Single-Mood	Walker-Lev Test 1	Walker-Lev Test 3	Double-Mood
Arrests (Continued)								
Antisystem	None recorded							
Political	.05	.04	−1.09	−4.91	.65	.00	6.31*	1.64*
Economic	−.03	.00	2.91	.00	.11	.06	.48	.28
Social	.01	.20	.37	−27.51	.20	1.84	.00	1.04
DELETED (m = 83; n = 28)								
Duration								
All events	−.04	.02	4.09	−.25	.26	1.43	3.87*	.72
Prosystem	−.01	.04	1.26	−2.84	.17	4.74*	4.60*	.24
Clashes	−.03	−.02	2.70	2.60	.36	.63	1.20	.71
Antisystem	−.00	.00	.13	.00	.13	.04	.10	.37
Political	−.00	.01	.48	−1.11	.32	1.44	.09	.55
Economic	−.02	−.01	2.26	.99	.12	.11	.05	.05
Social	−.02	.01	1.20	−.13	1.17	1.08	11.01*	1.84*
Deaths								
All events	−.03	−.03	2.30	3.70	.25	.00	5.88*	1.82*
Prosystem	−.01	−.01	.94	1.24	.27	.03	5.62*	1.68*
Clashes	−.02	−.62	1.37	2.47	.16	.00	2.21	1.14
Antisystem	None recorded							
Political	.00	.00	.02	.00	.12	.00	.20	.33
Economic	−.02	−.02	1.36	1.96	.20	.00	2.21	1.09
Social	−.01	−.01	.89	1.75	.20	.01	6.32*	1.97*
Arrests								
All events	−.05	.24	4.95	−21.49	.05	2.37	.47	.48
Prosystem	.00	.24	.86	−21.49	.18	3.33**	.18	.86
Clashes	−.05	.00	4.08	.00	.06	.14	.27	.15
Antisystem	None recorded							
Political	.00	.04	.33	.22	.77	.27	.18	
Economic	−.03	.00	3.07	.00	.07	.05	.00	.20
Social	−.02	.20	1.20	−18.30	.07	3.36**	.77	.52

*Significant at the .05 level
**Significant at the .10 level

and only prosystem violence had a significant (.05) slope change. All these changes were negative. There was a significant decrease in violent days per month in the postwar period. Recorded deaths associated with all events, prosystem, and social violence also demonstrated significant (.05) intercept changes. However, these were increases rather than decreases with no measurable slope differences. The number of arrests in the postwar period evidenced significant (.10) increases in slope for prosystem and social violence, but no significant slope changes occurred.

In conclusion, although there is a decrease in the duration of violence associated with World War II, an increase in deaths and arrests accompanies this decrease in days per month, indicating that the costs of violence rose. Prosystem and social violence are the most affected types of violence in this period.

KOREAN WAR

The impact of the Korean war, which the United States entered in June, 1950, was evaluated for seventy-five indicators (results Table 7.4). Twenty-four of these variables showed significant changes at the .05 level, and an additional thirteen at the .10 level. With the beginning of United States participation, the duration of domestic violence shows significant (.05) intercept increases for all events, clashes, antisystem, political, and economic violence accompanied by significant slope changes for every variable except political violence. Recorded deaths evidence significant (.10) intercept increases for all events, prosystem, political, economic violence, and antisystem violence was significant at this .05 level. All slope changes were minute, with only political (.10) and antisystem (.05) demonstrating a statistically significant decrease in direction. The number of arrests associated with prosystem and political violence demonstrate significant (.05) intercept increases, and the number of antisystem arrests evidence a significant (.05) decrease. The slope of the arrest lines shows no significant deviations.

The end of active fighting in Korea thirty-seven months later in July, 1953 evidences still further significant (.10) increases in the duration of political and economic violence. At this time prosystem violence also evidences a significant (.05) intercept increase and social violence a significant (.10) intercept decrease, with prosystem (.05), political (.10), and social (.05) violence demonstrating significant slope changes. Again recorded deaths rose significantly (.05) for all events and economic violence, with reaction events now also showing a significant increase in loss of life. Slopes remain unchanged. The only variable which has a significant (.05) change in the number of arrests at this time is prosystem violence, although there are relatively large rises in political and economic arrests and a decrease in arrests stemming from social violence.

The thirty-seven months of war were deleted and the quasi-

Table 7.4: Korean War

	Slope Pre	Slope Post	Intercept Pre	Intercept Post	Single-Mood	Walker-Lev Test 1	Walker-Lev Test 3	Double-Mood
START (m = 29; n = 79)								
Duration								
All events	.13	—.01	.04	2.37	1.04	12.08*	.08	2.40*
Prosystem	.00	—.01	.22	.87	1.17	.15	2.66	1.02
Clashes	.09	—.00	—.37	1.01	.89	10.18*	.14	2.30*
Antisystem	.05	.00	—.39	.11	1.54**	28.98*	5.72*	5.47*
Reaction	—.00	—.00	.58	.38	.42	.03	.35	.35
Prosystem and reaction	—.00	—.01	.81	1.25	.19	.04	.81	.57
Political	.00	—.01	.41	1.35	.72	.19	4.37*	1.35**
Economic	.13	.00	—.98	.16	1.09	32.43*	8.07*	6.09*
Social	.01	—.00	.61	.86	.73	.07	.11	.09
Deaths								
All events	.01	—.00	.02	.11	.65	1.45	.51	1.31**
Prosystem	.00	.00	.00	.08	I	.17	3.33**	1.16
Clashes	.00	.00	.06	.02	.33	.10	.50	.75
Antisystem	.01	.00	—.06	—.00	.67	4.12*	1.15	2.12*
Reaction	.00	.00	.02	.01	.24	.11	.25	.59
Prosystem and reaction	.00	—.00	.02	.09	.24	.26	.41	.18
Political	.01	—.00	—.06	.03	.67	2.98**	.08	1.38**
Economic	.01	.00	—.02	—.02	.39	.77	1.10	1.37**
Social	.00	.00	.10	.10	.14	.05	.07	.35
Arrests								
All events	.04	—.07	1.56	11.27	.41	.06	1.67	.85
Prosystem	—.08	—.05	2.19	5.78	.04	.03	4.82*	1.82*
Clashes	.07	—.01	—.38	5.40	.55	.04	.63	.49
Antisystem	.05	—.00	.24	.09	.43	2.32	1.18	1.18*
Reaction	None recorded							
Prosystem and reaction	—.08	—.05	2.19	5.78	.04	.03	4.82*	1.82*
Political	—.11	—.06	2.50	5.66	.34	.38	8.76*	2.69*
Economic	.15	.00	—.94	1.44	.64	.46	.00	.48
Social	.00	—.01	.00	4.16	I	.00	.57	.56
END (m = 67; n = 41)								
Duration								
All events	—.00	—.00	2.03	1.80	.35	.00	.03	.17
Prosystem	.00	—.02	.28	2.55	.76	4.22*	.17	1.18
Clashes	.00	.02	.86	—.63	.11	.68	.42	.91
Antisystem	—.00	.00	.26	.29	.23	.01	.01	.04
Reaction	—.01	.01	.63	—.40	.90	1.63	.05	.29
Prosystem and reaction	—.00	.02	.91	2.15	.20	.61	.23	.74
Political	.00	—.03	.54	2.72	.60	2.75**	.13	.97
Economic	—.01	—.03	.69	2.62	.51	1.34	1.07	1.40**
Social	.00	.05	.80	—3.55	.64	8.38*	2.67	2.68*

*Significant at the .05 level
**Significant at the .10 level

Table 7.4: Korean War (Continued)

	Slope Pre	Slope Post	Intercept Pre	Intercept Post	Single-Mood	Walker-Lev Test 1	Walker-Lev Test 3	Double-Mood
END (Continued) (m = 67; n = 41)								
Deaths								
All events	—.00	—.01	.17	.60	2.43*	.49	.76	1.07
Prosystem	.00	.00	.02	.00	.10	.00	.10	.32
Clashes	—.00	—.00	.09	.09	.18	.00	.03	.14
Antisystem	—.00	—.00	.02	.18	.05	.56	.56	.98
Reaction	—.00	—.00	.04	.33	8.00*	2.03	2.26	1.94*
Prosystem and reaction	—.00	—.00	.06	.33	5.62*	1.27	1.08	1.40**
Political	.00	—.00	.07	.18	.30	.99	.08	.11
Economic	—.00	—.00	.07	.41	3.98*	.57	1.92	1.57**
Social	—.00	.00	.10	.01	.09	.17	.02	.02
Arrests								
All events	.12	.08	1.65	—1.77	.54	.02	.98	.85
Prosystem	.06	—.06	.32	5.63	.67	2.33	4.10*	1.29**
Clashes	.06	.14	.86	—7.75	.34	.09	.21	.54
Antisystem	—.01	—.00	.46	.34	.01	.03	.12	.24
Reaction	None recorded							
Prosystem and reaction	.06	—.06	.32	5.63	.67	2.33	4.10*	1.29**
Political	.03	—.06	1.05	5.63	.53	1.77	1.53	.63
Economic	.09	—.09	—1.40	8.90	.43	1.55	1.00	.45
Social	.01	.22	1.72	—16.30	.15	.13	.04	.56
DELETED (m = 29; n = 41)								
Duration								
All events	.13	—.00	.04	1.71	1.56**	10.38*	3.92*	2.94*
Prosystem	.00	—.02	.22	1.68	.57	1.20	3.58**	1.50**
Clashes	.09	.02	—.37	—.04	1.56**	5.87*	5.32*	3.19*
Antisystem	.05	—.00	—.39	.20	1.54**	18.41*	7.31*	4.13*
Reaction	—.00	.01	.58	—.12	.51	.40	1.59	1.02
Prosystem and reaction	—.00	—.02	.81	1.56	.19	.25	.59	.59
Political	.00	—.03	.41	1.79	.53	.98	2.90**	1.35**
Economic	.13	—.03	—.98	1.67	1.09	26.84*	2.37	3.34*
Social	.01	.05	.61	—1.75	.73	3.14**	9.77*	2.54*
Deaths								
All events	.01	—.01	.02	.39	1.34**	2.02	.00	.43
Prosystem	None recorded							
Clashes	.00	—.00	.06	.08	.33	.10	.09	.38
Antisystem	.01	—.00	—.06	.11	.67	3.57**	.09	.83
Reaction	.00	—.00	.02	.20	4.70*	1.06	.82	.58
Political	.00	—.03	.40	1.79	.53	.98	2.90**	1.35**
Economic	.01	—.00	—.02	.37	2.10*	1.45	.11	.02
Social	—.00	.00	.10	.02	.14	.16	.11	.19

*Significant at the .05 level
**Significant at the .10 level

Table 7.4: Korean War (Continued)

	Slope		Intercept		Single-Mood	Walker-Lev		Double-Mood
	Pre	Post	Pre	Post		Test 1	Test 3	
DELETED (Continued) (m = 29; n = 41)								
Arrests								
All events	.04	.08	1.56	1.20	.41	.01	.01	.12
Prosystem	−.08	.06	2.19	3.47	.04	.11	2.56	1.62**
Clashes	.07	.14	−.38	−2.52	.55	.04	.00	.00
Antisystem	.05	−.00	−.24	.24	.43	1.29	.86	1.22**
Reaction	None recorded							
Political	−.12	.06	2.50	3.47	.34	1.12	5.63*	2.58*
Economic	.15	−.09	−.94	5.61	.64	2.15	.07	.16
Social	.00	.22	.00	−7.89	1	.37	.15	.20

*Significant at the .05 level
**Significant at the .10 level

experimental analysis indicates significantly different prewar and postwar periods concerning the magnitude and intensity of violence. The duration of violence is the most affected indicator. There is significant intercept increase evident in all events (.05), prosystem (.10), clashes (.05), antisystem (.05), political (.10), and economic (.05) violence, along with a significant decrease in social violence. Only reaction events demonstrate no deviation from the trend. In addition, all events (.05), clashes (.05), antisystem (.05), economic (.05), and social (.10) violence demonstrate significant slope changes. The number of recorded deaths are appreciably higher in the postwar period, with all events (.10), antisystem (.10), reaction (.05), and economic (.05) deaths each showing significant intercept increases. Only antisystem violence evidences any significant (.10) slope changes. It is interesting that there were no recorded prosystem deaths in the postwar period. The intercepts of the number of arrests rose significantly in the postwar period only for prosystem (.10), antisystem (.10), and political (.05) violence. It is noteworthy that while deaths increased for reaction events, there were no recorded arrests arising from reaction events in the postwar period. There are we conclude, significant differences in the pre-Korean war and post-Korean war periods, with most of these differences, unfortunately, in the direction of increases of duration and deaths associated with domestic violence.

THE VIETNAM WAR

The extensive buildup in American forces in Vietnam, undertaken in March 1965, has been selected as the starting point for the analysis of the impact of the Vietnam war on the pattern of domestic violence. The data base extends only to the end of 1970 and, thus, it will be possible to analyze the war's impact only for the beginning of the war (results Table 7.5). The analysis for this war consists of twenty-five indicators. Of these twenty-five, nine

Table 7.5: Vietnam War

	Slope Pre	Slope Post	Intercept Pre	Intercept Post	Single-Mood	Walker-Lev Test 1	Walker-Lev Test 3	Double-Mood
Duration								
All events	.14	.02	1.37	13.01	.02	1.13	1.05	.91
Prosystem	.02	—.00	.21	.21	1.02	2.37	.04	.03
Clashes	.09	—.04	.26	9.48	.40	5.23*	.64	.57
Antisystem	.02	.08	—.20	—1.50	.95	.96	1.01	1.10
Reaction	.02	—.03	1.10	4.23	.47	9.83*	.47	.37
Prosystem and reaction	.04	—.03	1.31	5.73	.88	9.17*	.30	.24
Political	.01	.05	—.09	—1.97	.79	4.39*	.66	1.04
Economic	.00	.00	.01	—.09	.19	.00	.59	.76
Social	.13	—.04	1.45	15.67	.04	2.36	.85	.76
Deaths								
All events	.02	—.15	.15	2.15	8.35*	.01	.71	.82
Prosystem	.00	.01	.00	—.43	R	.69	.04	.30
Clashes	.01	—.02	—.09	2.99	1.45**	.19	.65	.75
Antisystem	.00	.02	—.04	—.93	.58	.42	.02	.21
Reaction	.01	—.00	—.02	.62	4.75*	3.46**	.32	.37
Prosystem and reaction	.01	.00	—.02	.19	9.97*	.00	.19	.42
Political	.00	.01	—.01	—.59	.31	1.89	.78	.74
Economic	None recorded							
Social	.01	—.00	—.14	2.94	8.40*	.06	.89	.91
Arrests								
All events	1.20	1.57	34.44	—2.10	.57	.01	.01	.09
Prosystem	.81	—.08	4.20	20.94	.39	.95	1.07	1.13
Clashes	.51	.14	23.33	28.53	.47	.07	.09	.33
Antisystem	—.08	1.46	4.51	—47.32	.01	.21	.09	.35
Reaction	—.05	.04	2.40	—2.90	.15	4.19*	.04	.02
Prosystem and reaction	.76	—.03	6.61	16.69	.39	.74	1.11	1.14
Political	1.16	.91	—23.44	—50.86	.48	.09	1.77	1.35**
Economic	None recorded							
Social	.05	.66	57.88	48.76	.36	.03	.04	.21

*Significant at the .05 level
**Significant at the .10 level

were significant at the .05 level and an additional two at the .10 level. The duration of violent events rose significantly (.05) for the following types of events: clashes, reaction, and political violence. Clashes and reaction demonstrate significant intercept increases, which decrease for political violence, while slopes decrease significantly for clashes and reaction and increase for political violence. This would indicate that for the former two types of violence duration rose immediately and then slackened, while political violence increases during the war period. The number of deaths attributable to domestic violence increases significantly for a number of types of violence in the war period. All events (.05), clashes (.10), reaction (.05), and social (.05) deaths all show appreciable increases. These are, however, immediate increases. The levels then return to the trend begun before the war intensified, with slopes and intercepts for the entire period rising at the same rate as in the prewar period. The number of arrests is significantly altered only for reaction (.05) and political (.10) events. Both show decreases in intercept. The former shows an increase in slope and the latter a decrease. It is significant to note the almost nonexistence of economic violence as measured by duration and that no deaths or arrests associated with economic violence were recorded for the entire war period.

The Comparative Impact of the Five Wars

The five wars, while not evidencing comparability over all variables and types of violence for each of the war periods, do show a number of important similarities and step changes. At the start of all five wars there were significant intercept changes. The nature of these intercept changes, however, varies from period to period. When three of the wars (World War I, Korean and Vietnam) began, the duration of political organizational violence rose significantly, and in no case did political organizational violence significantly decrease. This occurred despite the fact that only in one war (Korean) did the total duration of all events increase at the start of the war. In the two largest wars, (World War I and World War II), the extent of economic violence decreased with their commencement, while at the start of the two smallest wars, (Korean, Spanish-American), economic violence, as measured by duration, rose. As was noted previously, there was almost no economic violence for the entire Vietnam war period. Social violence was only significantly affected in World War I and World War II, rising in the former and decreasing at first in the latter. In only the Korean war did duration of antisystem violence increase significantly, while clashes rose in the last three wars, decreased during World War I, and did not deviate during the Spanish-American War. Prosystem violence was only significantly altered at the start of World War I and World War II, rising in the former and decreasing in the latter. However, reaction, which we have classified as a private form of prosystem violence, also rose during the Vietnam war. When we compare changes in recorded deaths resulting from violent events at the start of war, there are a number of significant changes that occur only in the last three wars. No changes occur in the Spanish-American War or World War I. There were thirteen indicators for which there were three significant changes in the number of deaths recorded. Eleven of the thirteen indicators showed increases and only two (prosystem and economic-related deaths during World War II) demonstrated significant declines. The only consistent pattern emerges in the total number of deaths resulting from all events. This total rose in all three of the later wars. The variable arrests when significantly altered rises on all occasions, except for antisystem arrests during the Korean war. Excluding the Spanish-American War, when no significant changes occur in arrests, arrests resulting from political violence increase at the start of all the wars. Prosystem arrests rose at the start of World War I, World War II, and during the Korean war.

When we compare the four completed wars for the impact that the end of active participation had on domestic violence, we find, within each war period, much greater consistency in the direction of impact than at the onset of war, across all three variables of magnitude and intensity. With the exceptions of World War II, where prosystem and economic duration evidence the only significant deviations, and of economic duration following the Korean war, all remaining significant deviations move in an upward direction. The most affected postwar period is that of World War I, when the extent of every type of violence increases. Political violence, which rose significantly at the beginning of World War I and the Korean war, is significantly increased in postwar periods as well.

The costs of domestic violence, as indicated by number of deaths, evidences no decreases with the end of war. In the Spanish-American War there was no measurable deviation, but for the other three wars deaths, when deviating from the war period trend, only increase. World War I once again demonstrates the most marked impact. Arrests provide a pattern that is closer to duration than deaths at the end of the wars. While there are no significant changes after the Spanish-American War, arrests after World War I are appreciably higher and then fall, as did duration after World War II. The only affected type of arrest after the Korean war was prosystem arrests which, like duration, significantly increased. It is noteworthy that this follows upon the heels of an increase in arrests at the start of the war.

When the four war periods were deleted, there were significant step level increases in the number of days per month when violence took place in the postwar periods of the Spanish-American War, World War I, and the Korean war, and decreases associated with World War II. The post-World War I and Korean war periods evidence increases in duration of all types of violence, with the exception of social violence following the Korean war. While all types of violence do not evidence significant increases following the Spanish-American War, it should be emphasized that there was not enough recorded prosystem or antisystem violence to statistically analyze that postwar period for those types of violence. The number of deaths attributable to domestic violence shows only significant increases when deviation from prewar periods occurs in the postwar months for both World War II and the Korean war. Despite the fact that for World War II the duration of all violence, prosystem and social violence significantly decreased, deaths for these types of violence increased in the postwar periods.

The hypothesis that, after each of the wars, the postevent distribution of domestic violence was part of either a seasonal or a longer term trend does not appear tenable, because the prewar observations do not exhibit the same trend. It is clearly not the case that preevent values can be extrapolated to obtain the results evidenced. Much of the postwar behavior appears to be part of a different trend—that is, sensitive to different forces than was prewar behavior. In the second half of this chapter we will explore these aberrations.

Evaluation of Hypotheses

Three substantive hypotheses were explicated earlier predicting changes in the postwar interactions and behavior. While the quasi-experimental approach does not allow inferences to be drawn in terms of strength of relationship, changes in the pattern of violence in terms of these hypotheses may be indicated.

> *Hypothesis 1:* Wartime economic mobilization brings new groups into the productive process and enhances the economic positions of groups relative to the dominant segments thus intensifying economic conflict and violence.

After both the start and end of the Spanish-American War the number of days of economic violence increased. However, after the start of World War I economic violence fell, although it rose again after the Armistice. Link (1966: 309) points out that the average number of strikes during the period 1916-1921 was 3,503 per year and that during 1919 there were 2,665 strikes involving more than four million workers (Link, 1966: 234). Despite the growth of strikes, the level of violence during World War I was low, and the violence was mainly directed against strikers. The increase in violence after 1919 may be explained by the twin factors of the government's postwar policy of sending troops to trouble spots as a precautionary measure, and by the fact that employers, who had accepted the tremendous union growth (from 2,772,000 to 4,881,000 during 1916-1921) as a wartime necessity or a government fiat, were now anxious to rid themselves of labor organizations (Taft and Ross, 1969: 332-333). At the start of World War II economic violence decreased, as it did at the start of World War I. The forty-five months of American War participation, however, witnessed the greatest number of strikes of any period up until that time—14,471 strikes involving 6,774,000 workers. The bulk of these strikes were over working conditions and not wages, however, and both the union leadership and management worked to suppress the strikes. There was, thus, a decrease in violence (see Brecher, 1972). The end of the war saw an even greater acceleration of strikes. The number of work days lost to strikes doubled in September and then doubled again in

October, yet, the increase in strikes notwithstanding, the duration of violence decreased, although the costs of violence rose, with deaths significantly increasing in the postwar period. The war had integrated the American economy more than ever before and accelerated the acceptance of labor as a junior partner, a process which had been formalized with the passage of the Wagner Act in 1935. A normalization and deintensification of conflict in labor-management relations was expected from this time forward. But employers, who in 1919 had attempted to break the union growth of World War I, now fought for and received the Taft-Hartley Bill, which attempted to return labor to its proper junior role by reducing the unions' powers as stipulated by the Wagner Act.

At the start of the Korean war economic violence again increased and continued significantly upward with the war's conclusion. During the war itself, there was one major steel strike, in which President Truman briefly seized the mills until his action was reversed by the Supreme Court. The strike continued for fifty-four days, but no major violence or deaths were recorded. After the immediate postwar period labor-management relations improved, and there has been little economic violence since the immediate postwar period. The Vietnam war period is the only case where no significant change in economic violence occurred, and since 1960 there have been no deaths recorded in the data set attributable to economic violence. Thus, it appears that the four earliest wars accelerated economic violence by increasing labor's bargaining position and enhancing management's negative reaction to new demands. Organized labor was eventually accepted, however, as a respectable partner, and by the period of the Vietnam war, unions and management were working conspicuously together to protect their ever more similar interests.

Hypothesis 2: Wartime social mobility increases status positions of underdog social groups, relative to the dominant segments which increases hostilities between them.

Both the initiation of the Spanish-American War and the end of fighting brought no change in social violence. It should be stressed that the last sixteen years of the nineteenth century witnessed more than 2,500 lynchings of blacks and that from 1900-1914 there were an additional 1,100 black victims (Link, 1966: 31). It should also be noted that the period before the Spanish-American War witnessed very high levels of nativist violence. While these did not increase in the post Spanish-American War period, nativists did once again display "symptoms of hysteria and violence" by 1914 (Higham, 1967: 183). Higham posits that the acquisition of an empire after the Spanish-American War fortified the confidence of dominant segments renewed by prosperity after the war. They gained confidence from relief from class conflict and from a psychologically invigorating war, and this accounted for the decline of nativism until 1914 (Higham, 1967: 108). The initiation and conclusion of World War I were accompanied by significant increases in social violence. During World War I the cities of the north saw their black populations increase in large numbers as blacks moved north, primarily due to the growing demand for labor. While the war continued there were an increasing number of racial incidents. With the end of the war, the decrease in available jobs, and the frequent use of blacks as strikebreakers, social hostilities increased markedly, and culminated in major race riots in Chicago, Charleston, Washington, Knoxville, Omaha, and Long View, Texas. In each of these riots, whites attacked blacks. In addition, during the war German-Americans in Montana, Minnesota, and Wisconsin were whipped, tarred, and feathered as part of the war hysteria. The conclusion of the war saw ethnic hatred transferred to alien radicals (see discussion of Hypothesis 3).

The start of World War II was also accompanied by massive migration of blacks from the south to the urban industrial centers. Racial hostilities did not wait for the war's conclusion in this case, with major riots occurring in Detroit, Los Angeles, and Harlem. As noted previously, the Detroit and Los Angeles riots followed the pattern of 1919 and other preceding race riots, but the Harlem violence was mainly directed at white property and was initiated by blacks. While World War II witnessed far less violence than World War I, there was a greater increase in black militancy (see Dalfiume, 1971: 148). At the end of the war there was a decrease in duration of racial violence, but an increase in deaths. In contrast to World War I, where blacks threatened white jobs, the end of World War II saw blacks lose jobs far more quickly than whites, and the postwar period, despite the increase in strikes, was one of relative prosperity. German-Americans were not the victims of nativist hysteria as in World War I; instead the government instituted its own version of racial hysteria by detaining 110,000 Japanese-Americans in stockades for most of the war's duration.

During the Korean war period America witnessed no increase in racial or ethnic violence. The Supreme Court's *Brown* v. *The Board of Education* decision came almost a year after the conclusion of the war, and was not followed by an upsurge in violence for another year. This violent white reaction was not directly attributable to the war, although the war did help accelerate the rise in black status through the desegregation of the armed services, finally completed in 1955 (see Quarles, 1964: 235). The Vietnam war period provides an interesting surprise in that there appears to be no increase in the duration of social violence attributable to the war. Only deaths due to social violence deviate from the prewar trend providing increased human costs without increased duration. The rise in black-white violence, largely characterized by black "commodity riots" (see Janowitz, 1969), was part of a long term trend that began before the acceleration of the war effort. There is a significant increase in government-initiated violence against black radical groups but this was more properly subsumed under the political organization category. Thus, only the two world wars significantly altered the pattern of social violence. It is difficult to ascribe the racial difficulties of the past ten years to the Vietnam war, as many analysts have done. According to the data contained herein the Vietnam war did not appear to influence that pattern either positively or negatively.

Hypothesis 3: The economic and social changes of the war generate demands for the reallocation of political power and rewards which intensifies conflict and violence between top and bottom.

Corollary A: Success in war provides increased goods to be distributed by dominant segments while increasing their power and prestige. This intensifies their efforts to maintain the control of the political system while increasing their ability to do so. The result is an increase in violence directed downward by dominant segments which is greater than the increase of lower segment.

Corollary B: Lack of success in war decreases the power and prestige of dominant segments and provides no additional goods to distribute.

This intensifies their efforts to maintain control of the political system without increasing their ability to do so. The result is an increase in violence directed downward which is matched by an increase in violence directed upward by lower segments attempting to maintain the relative gains accrued to them during war.

As indicated earlier, there were no changes in political violence after the Spanish-American War and not enough recorded government-initiated violent events for analysis. During and after World War I the picture is quite different, with a sharp increase in both prosystem and political violence, as well as a small increase in antisystem initiated violence at the end of the war. The great increase in violence can be traced to the legislative and ideological foundations laid during the war for a nationalistic antiradical crusade. This crusade included legislation: the Espionage Act of 1917, the Sedition Act of 1918, and the congressional authorization, in 1918, of the Justice and Labor Departments' right to deport any alien simply on grounds of his membership in an organization which advocated revolt or sabotage. No such bills were passed in the Spanish-American War, perhaps because of the swift success of the war effort. As a result of the World War I legislation over 2,100 persons were prosecuted under the alien and sedition acts but only ten of them for actual sabotage (Link, 1966: 212). In addition, the red scare of 1919-1920 and the resultant Palmer raids led to the arrest of over 4,000 persons, including bona fide citizens, most of whom were eventually released after spending time in government stockades. However, 556 aliens were deported simply for being Communist party members.

World War II witnessed an initial decrease in the level of prosystem violence as measured by duration and deaths, but an increase in arrests. Arrests associated with political violence also increased. It was indicated in Chapter 6 that there was little opposition to the war once the Japanese had attacked Pearl Harbor and with the exception of the internment of Japanese-Americans and trouble arising in the stockades in which they were held, there was no recorded violence. At the end of the war the level of political violence duration decreases, but the slope or direction of the violence is upward after the initial decrease in the postwar period. Deaths attributable to prosystem violence increases after the war, while arrests associated with political and prosystem violence decrease markedly with the armistice only to increase once again in time. The government's efforts to protect the nation from internal radicals and alien subversive were not as spectacular as in the previous war. However, Truman's Attorney General, Tom Clark, began to deport aliens who were considered communists shortly after assuming his new position. In February, 1947, he reported that 124 people had been deported on the grounds that they were communists (Freeland, 1972: 217). In March of that year President Truman issued an executive order establishing the Federal Employee Loyalty Program, which involved an unprecedented use of background information and screening procedures for all current and future federal employees. In the spring and summer of 1947, Attorney General Clark compiled a list of subversive organizations. "The list was nothing more than a public designation by the attorney general of organizations operating within the United States that he considered 'communist,' 'fascist,' 'totalitarian,' or 'subversive'... the list immediately demonstrated a capacity to undermine the political effectiveness of cited organizations" (Freeland, 1972: 208). Thus while the magnitude of deportation activities and the public and governmental reaction in no way approached the hysteria of 1919-1920, the same processes of fear and curtailment of civil liberties were set in motion. It should also be noted that the raw files collected under the loyalty program provided the material for McCarthy's later unsubstantiated charges of communist infiltration in the federal government.

The period preceding the Korean war has been characterized as "a period of greater peacetime repression that the country had ever known" (Brooks, 1969: 514). The Republican Congress and President Truman competed to see who could root out the most subversives from the government. We have already indicated Truman's executive tools used to protect the government from disloyal and subversive employees. The Congress utilized the congressional investigating committee, with special notoriety accruing to the House Un-American Activities Committee, and also instituted restrictive and legally questionable legislation, most notably the McCarran-Walter Immigration Bill and the Internal Security Act of 1950. The former was favorable primarily to the immigration of Northern Europeans with the virtual exclusion of peoples from all other areas of the globe. In addition, "communists and subversives were barred from admission to the United States, but no such provisions were imposed on Nazis, Fascists and Falangists" (Cook, 1971: 320). The Internal Security Act established a five-man Subversive Activities Control Board and provided registration requirements and mechanisms for communists and other subversives. It also established a half dozen concentration camps which could be used under proclamation of emergency.

Against this background, the start of the Korean war produced still higher levels of political violence. Antiwar violence did not account for this increase, having been successfully eliminated through fear and prowar violence at the onset of the war (see Chapter 6). Antisystem violence increased at this time, while the end of the war brought with it even greater duration levels of prosystem and political violence. Joseph McCarthy, who symbolizes the hysteria of the period, began his rise to notoriety four months prior to the outbreak of the war. He was restrained somewhat, however, by a Democratic Congress. With the Republican Congressional victory in the fall of 1952, McCarthy assumed the chairmanship of the previously innocuous Committee of Government Operations. The end of the war coincided with the acceleration of his activities. McCarthy's attacks and "investigations" do not fall directly into the categories of political violence collected for analysis, but the whole range of governmental activity is important because, against this background of congressional and executive activity, prosystem violent events increased as well.

The start of the Vietnam war brought increased political and reaction violence as measured by duration, deaths, and arrests. While much of the violence during the war can be characterized as antiwar and antisystem, this antisystem bias did not begin to equal prowar violence until October of 1967. With the increases in antiwar group initiated violence, however, came corresponding prosystem increases, as the events of Chicago, in August, 1968 and Kent State, in May, 1970, bear witness. It is also important to remember that the antiwar violence was directed primarily toward property, while prosystem violence was aimed at individuals. Employing the provisions of the Internal Security Act of 1950, the Nixon administration was responsible for the internment of 10,000 demonstrators in Robert F. Kennedy stadium during and after the May Day demonstrations of 1971. The Watergate hearings also revealed the existence of extensive governmental preparations for handling "subversives" and the administration appears to have had plans for linking the Democrats to the "communist menace," a plan McCarthy, Nixon, and the Republicans were able to sell the public twenty years ago.

Thus, with each of the last four wars discussed, violence between top and bottom increased, and dominant segments perceived a direct challenge to their authoritative positions and to the political system itself. In World War I and World War II, where war aims were clearly achieved, it was predicted that prosystem violence would be greater than antisystem violence. While we can not evaluate the strength of this relationship, it is clear that in World War I the increase in prosystem violence was far greater than the increase in antisystem violence. However, in World War II both forms of violence decrease with the war's end, and prosystem violence began an immediate rise, a trend that does not characterize antisystem violence. Although the Korean and Vietnam wars certainly did not have successful outcomes, with the conclusion of the Korean war there was a rise in prosystem violence, much greater than antisystem violence, which appears to refute corollary B of hypothesis 3. Vietnam's postwar period has not been analyzed, but if current trends continue, there does not seem to be much support for corollary B in this case either.

In conclusion, it should be stressed that the quasi-experimental approach located step-level changes in violence in the postwar periods following all the wars. In spite of the mixed results in supporting the three hypotheses, the importance of comparing prewar and postwar years for changes in violence due to involvement in war is highlighted by a comparison with the results of a study by Sheldon Levy (1969: 83) which found that

> The absolute number of politically violent events has been rising throughout American history with the exception of three periods. One was in the decade prior to the turn of the century. The second was prior to and following World War One. This was followed by a sharp rise during the depression period but there was another drop shortly before, through and shortly after the Second World War.

Increases in postwar violence also appear to occur during periods which are not characterized by long term increases in violence. An approach which did not have the ability to distinguish short term slope and intercept changes would likely miss a substantial change within these long term trends. In the concluding chapter we will consider some plausible rival hypotheses and indicate a number of additional research possibilities.

NOTES

1. For each of the time series analyses concerning the start and end of war, each month preceding the experimental input comprised the pretest series and each month after the event, the posttest series. When the war months are deleted the pretest series remains the same as at the start of the war, but the posttest series does not commence until after the cessation of hostilities. We thus actually eliminate all months during which the war was fought and directly compare the prewar and postwar months.

2. The difference in the number of variables analyzed for each of the wars results from: (1) the absence of certain types of behavior in the five periods, for example during the Spanish-American War period, there were only 16 recorded prosystem events and none between 1894-1900 (after the Homestead and Pullman strikes). There were 21 recorded antisystem initiated events with most occurring after 1901. For both of these categories there were many more observation points than events which this prevented statistical analysis. And (2) the addition after World War II of the categories of reaction and prosystem and reaction, with the former referring to private forms of prosystem behavior and the latter representing the combined prosystem category in previous war periods. The prosystem violence for the latter two wars thus simply refers to government-initiated violence.

3. The intercepts indicate the initial value in the series, i.e., the measurement of the variable at time point x_m, for the pretest series and x_n in the posttest series.

Chapter 8

ASSESSMENTS, EXTENSIONS, AND INTENSIONS OF THE STUDY OF EXTERNAL-INTERNAL VIOLENCE LINKAGES

Introduction

This study was conceived as an effort which would contribute to a theory of political violence. The particular purpose of the work was to examine the impact of war on domestic political violence in the United States. It was asserted that there was a need for a reexamination of this relationship, because there were both theoretical and methodological problems which had prevented a proper evaluation. In Chapters 2 and 3, we reviewed the literature concerning political violence, conflict and aggression, and the study of linkages between foreign and domestic conflict behavior, and highlighted these theoretical and methodological problems. Chapters 4 and 5 attempted to correct past limitations, and offered a theoretical and methodological design which would allow refutation of the basic relationship and its corollaries.

Along the way, a number of assumptions were stated concerning crucial conceptual issues in the study of political violence. It was asserted that to properly study domestic violence, it was necessary to examine violence perpetrated by agents acting for, or in support of, the political system as well as violence committed by agents acting against the system and its supporters. It was thus particularly important to assess the role of governmental agencies in violent events. It will be remembered that violence committed by, or in the name of the state, was not discussed as violence in most previous studies, but rather as conflict management. We rejected this position and asserted that it is necessary that a theory of violence consider all collective violent events, regardless of their source. We therefore characterized the various governmental structures as partisan factions rather than as neutral conflict managers. We found (Chapter 6) overwhelming support for this position, because 95% of the recorded cases of government initiation and intervention in violent events were against subordinate segments.

This relationship became particularly important when we examined the impact of war on domestic violence (Chapter 7) and found that political organizational violence was the most affected indicator of domestic violence during and after war, and most of the changes in this indicator were in the area of prosystem initiated violence. Thus, if we had followed the conceptualization of previous studies, we probably would have found little support for this most important linkage, even with methodological innovations.

We also stressed the need to isolate violent events in which physical attacks actually took place from the traditional category of conflict behavior. This latter designation, in previous studies, was composed of all actions of groups confronting the state and therefore included strikes and demonstrations against government and dominant segments even when violence did not actually occur, or was not actually initiated by the antisystem groups who were peacefully demonstrating or striking. While we did not collect data on all conflict behavior and record all nonviolent demonstrations, strikes, etc., we did digress shortly in Chapter 6 to examine "antiwar" violence and found that the historical record clearly indicated that most "antiwar" violence, particularly before October, 1967, was primarily nonviolent and when violence did occur it was typically the result of prowar groups and government agents attacking protesters.

The two world wars witnessed large scale strike waves at their conclusion, yet violence associated with labor-management relations actually decreased following World War II and did not increase at nearly the same rate as did violence following World War I. The major difference between the two periods is accounted for by the knowledge that employers attacked strikers with the purpose of breaking their recently established union strength after World War I, often with governmental assistance, while after World War II, when labor unions had their rights formally legalized by the Wagner Act, 1935, management turned to less violent methods and lobbied for the Taft-Hartley Act, a bill antilabor congressmen were quite willing to support. The Korean war, however, offers a contrary example, in that while strikes did not significantly increase with the war's conclusion, economic violence did significantly rise. Thus, peaceful and violent strikes do not appear to exhibit the same trend, and while obviously not independent, these findings suggest that factors responsible for the violence of strikes differ from the causes of the strikes themselves. To paraphrase Ronald Steel (1973: 29), the interesting and important question is not necessarily who caused the violence. The search for cause in politics may be as elusive as it is in theology. Rather, the interesting question is why the confrontations took the forms that they did. To examine these forms we employed the interrupted time series quasi-experimental design and we will now turn to an examination of its limitations and strengths.

Quasi-Experimental Analysis and the Study of Linkages

The quasi-experimental analysis indicated that war did have a significant, although differing impact on the pattern of domestic violence for each of the five wars. The design does have important limitations despite its ability to locate deviations from trend, both short and long term. The three most important limitations have been discussed by Caporaso (1973) and concern the lack of a measure of strength of association, the atheoretical nature of quasi-experiments, and their nontransactional nature. We shall now confront each of these limitations.

As was indicated, the evaluation of whether the experiment input had an effect on the dependent variable is limited to data inspection and the use of tests of significance. "Thus while we possess a measure of the improbability of a certain effect we have little cue as to how strong the relationship" (Caporaso, 1973: 25). We have looked at the magnitude of the intercept and slope changes to obtain a rough estimate of the strength of relationship for a number of the important linkages. However, no statistical method of evaluating strength was available. Thus, we are limited to suggesting that war had certain impacts, as indicated by improbable or nonrandom deviations, but we can not say with any certainty how strong these relationships between internal and external variables are, except by indicating the frequency of deviation.

The second problem, the criticism that quasi-experiments are atheoretical, appears much less serious. The critique asserts that in the analysis we are simply observing what has happened with the introduction of the event. If the event appears to have an effect or not, that is all we have been able to ascertain, and therefore no theoretical conclusions can be drawn. Critics thus suggest "for this reason these findings might add to our factual knowledge (which is already voluminous) but not to a cumulative body of theory" (Caporaso, 1973: 26). This seems a very narrow conception of the theory building process. The results obtained in this, or any other, quasi-experimental or experimental study, might indeed add to a more informed theoretical discussion of the causes of violence within societies by indicating the need to account for the change in process of violence during and after war. Thus, a theory of political violence must confront this evidence and broaden its scope to include the effect of external influences. If this were done, then the approach would certainly have had important theoretical impact.

The final limitation, that of the nontransactional nature of quasi-experimentation, is only serious if one were to rely solely on this procedure for both construction and testing of theoretical models. The design cannot detect the strength of feedback and the interactive nature of variables, and indeed, one of the assumptions of the interrupted time series analysis is that the event takes place independently of the values of the dependent variable. Therefore, strict reliance on this method could result in misleading conclusions concerning the causal relationships involved. If the design is used, as suggested above, to test particular relationships, either from a deductive model, or a set of loose hypotheses, then other more appropriate methodologies, such as path analysis may be employed to detect feedback and evaluate entire theoretical constructions.

Extensions and Intensions of the Linkage Variables

As was stated in Chapter 5, the tests of the hypotheses of necessity ignored much of the complexity of the environment within which the events occurred. There are obviously a great number of events which took place coterminously with participation in war and which may plausibly rival war as an explanation of the changes that were evidenced. The corrective for this problem suggested in Chapter 5 was good theory and cross-case comparison. There is one particular "cause" that is often referred to in the literature explaining the repression that has followed United States participation in World War I, World War II, and the Korean war—the perceived threat of Russian communism and the need to protect the United States from Soviet aggression. In light of the results of the quasi-experimental analysis, the strongest case for this proposition appears to be in the political consequences of this threat and the fact that the search for enemies has consistently been limited to leftwing groups. However, this proposition ignores the changes that occur in social and economic violence, unless we extend the search for enemies and the roots of all American economic and social problems to the instigation of foreign controlled subversives. Despite the great time and effort expended by governmental agencies and reactionary groups, virtually no factual basis for the latter assertions have been produced. In fact, even in the case of the governmental sphere, the internal search for enemies following World War II and during and after the Korean war uncovered fewer than fifty employees in the Federal government—from a pool of over two and a half million—who were in any way considered to even be disloyal.

However, this does not imply that we should quickly dismiss this "plausible" hypothesis, since there is always a gap between evidence and its perception. Fear exists and lingers despite its irrationality. The best means to test the relationship between threats to the international status quo and the internal search for enemies would be to extend the analysis to a number of other nations and their war and postwar experiences. There is, for example, evidence that Great Britain reacted to the French Revolution and the Napoleonic Wars, during the late eighteenth and early nineteenth century, in much the same fashion as the United States reacted to the Russian Revolution and the wars of the twentieth century. However, the British did not experience the same hysteria following the wars of this century. We suggest, therefore, that reaction may in large part be dependent upon the changing position of the nation in the international status hierarchy; both the United States and Britain reacted quite vigorously when they were at the top of that hierarchy, but Britain appears not to react with her decline in status. Therefore, in future studies, an extension of the data set should include the addition of the international status hierarchy as an intervening variable.

An increase in the number of nations and wars considered would also allow additional research designs that would be capable of statistically assessing cross variable time-series analysis. The independent variable could then be more profitably measured for different characteristics rather than as simply an interruption point. Durkheim, for example, in his study *Suicide* (1951: 206-207) suggests that "while great national wars have had a strong influence on the current of suicide in both France and Germany, purely dynastic wars such as the Crimean or Italian, which have not violently moved the masses, have had no appreciable effect." This would suggest a number of important measures of war that should be examined for their impact, i.e., length, scope, casualties, domestic popularity, and social distance of the adversary from the nation under study. In addition, the success or failure of the war in question should also be assessed. In the present work, we merely differentiated between degrees of success, and perhaps this led to the inconclusiveness of the analysis on this point. There are a number of nations, which although defeated on the battlefield, were left as independent political entities at the peace table. It is logical that defeat in battle would significantly lower the power and prestige of dominant groups, and thus while we would expect them to struggle to maintain their control of the political system, we would also expect greater opposition to the continuance of their dominance from within.

Having identified the modifications in the independent variable that would contribute to further understanding of the relationship between war and its domestic consequences, it should be noted that war was originally chosen to test the existence of the external-internal linkage primarily because it was considered to be the most extreme destabilizing external influence. Now that we have demonstrated the existence of such a relationship, we would suggest that the independent variable be extended to include less extreme "external" inputs such as crisis, intervention, and other major foreign policy decisions in descending order of their likely impact.

There are intensions of the dependent variable that ought also to be considered. The most important of these would involve gathering additional data and constructing indicators of the process of violence and its management during the violent events. It would be particularly germane to the study of the impact of war if we were able to determine whether the instigation of violence and reactions to violence by both prosystem and antisystem segments changed during and after war. In addition, an examination of statutory changes for official reactions to violence and alterations of the legal status of collective behavior, whether in protest or support of governmental policy, should prove quite fruitful.

End Note: The American Capacity for Repression

Having been especially careful up to this point not to draw any hard and fast conclusions or to assert the verification of any scientific laws, we now feel compelled before ending to state some conclusions less strictly anchored in the scientific method.

Twice in the past fifty-five years the American people have witnessed what are commonly referred to as red scares. The first scare (1919-1920) is generally recalled only by scholars of the period. The second, familiar to many as the McCarthy era, while not forgotten, is considered by most who remember it as simply an aberration, the result of the unfortunate and random elevation to power of a hysterical caricature of his time. It is forgotten how little opposition there was to McCarthy's goals and methods and how much support he was able to generate both among the American people and their elected representatives. At the outset of McCarthy's rise to notoriety, "Mr. Republican," Robert Taft, the symbol for many of integrity, counseled McCarthy to create an issue that would catch on, and suggested that that issue be communism and loyalty.

It was only when McCarthy went to extremes and began to attack the dominant groups, most notably the army, that those who had quietly acquiesced in his excesses began to challenge him directly. Before this fatal army attack, the then Vice-President of the United States, Richard Nixon, actively worked behind the scenes to encourage the President and his cabinet to allow McCarthy to do the necessary dirty work, while the White House and congressional leaders remained aloof as symbols of virtue.

When in 1968, amid the turmoil and alienation produced by the Vietnam war, Richard Nixon was elected President, he began to establish the necessary conditions for a third Red scare. During the first Nixon Administration the cornerstone was laid with the appointment of John Mitchell as Attorney General. The foundation was built up by the establishment of a secret "investigating" force (the Plumbers) and the perversion of the concept of law and order, with the emphasis on order at the expense of law in general and due process in particular. This concern for order parallels the early stages of the previous scare.

The actual scare itself, we may conclude, was scheduled to commence in the early months of the second term. The Watergate investigations revealed secret memos composed in February, 1973, which detail a new Nixon attempt to connect the Democratic Party and anyone else who opposed the President's actions or inaction with "communists and other foreign subversives." That this was not merely an election tactic (apparently to most commentators that would have been more forgiveable given Nixon's previous electoral behavior), but a postelection plan is indicative of how close the nation came to a new wave of hysteria. Fortuitously, the executors of the scare were forced to shelve the plan while they attempted to extricate themselves from the political and legal difficulties arising out of the investigations of the Watergate burglary. They were unsuccessful, and thus the nation was spared the trauma of another internal search for enemies.

This brings us to two observations, separated by almost one hundred and forty years, concerning the impact of war on political systems.

> All those who seek to destroy the liberties of a democratic nation ought to know that war is the surest and shortest means to accomplish it [Alexis deTocqueville, 1954: 284].

> Wars are invariably followed by periods of reaction and repressiveness, and the emergency powers yielded to the executive in wartime are never subsequently restored in their entirety to the people or the legislature [J. William Fulbright, 1972: 178].

Thus, while there is not unqualified support for these two observations contained in this study, varying support is evidenced by three of the four completed wars, and the possibilities of the fourth war resulting in the same repressive and reactionary response may have just narrowly been averted. We submit that there is therefore an additional argument here for the lunacy of war— even for the so-called victors and noncombatants, and that if moral arguments hold no sway with the members of the "realist" school who have dominated foreign policy in the major nations in the post-World War II period, perhaps the reality of this threat should become more well-known. If not, the Orwellian argument of obtaining domestic and international peace through war and violence will certainly continue to be advocated.

APPENDIX I

TESTS OF SIGNIFICANCE*

Single-Mood Test

The single-mood test is a t-test appropriate for assessment of the deviation of the first value after the occurrence of an event from a theoretical value predicted by an extrapolation from a linear fit of pre-X values. As pointed out elsewhere, (Caporaso and Pelowski, 1971) it is a simple line-fitting technique based on the least-squared criterion where the regression estimate of the pre-X data is used to predict the first observation value. The t statistic yields a value indicating the probability that the observed value could have occurred simply by extrapolating the line. The single-mood test is suited for distributions of the following type:

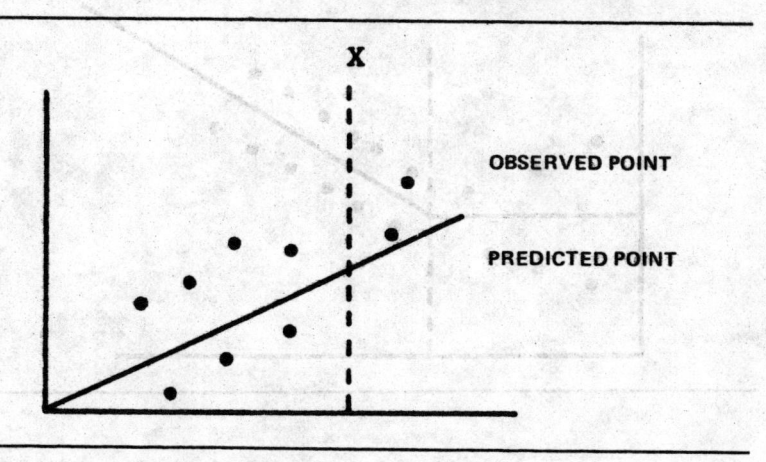

---

* Source: Caporaso, James and Roos, Leslie, *Quasi-Experimental Approaches.*

Double-Mood Test

This test simply extends the logic of the single-mood test. It involves both a pre-X and post-X linear fit and a comparison of the predictions by these two estimates of a hypothetical value lying midway between the last pre-X point and the first post-X point (Sween and Campbell, 1965: 6). This test is appropriate for the assessment of intercept differences as well as slope changes.

INTERCEPT DIFFERENCE

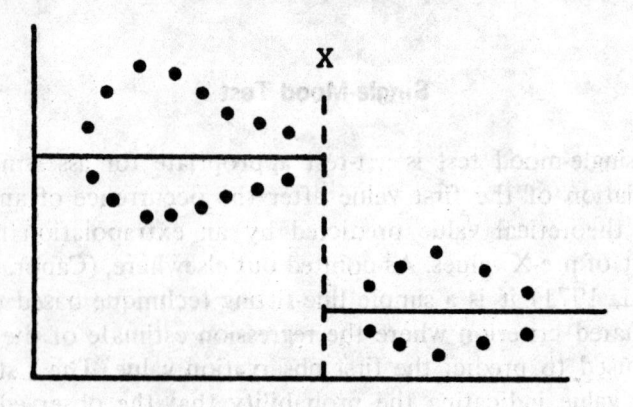

SLOPE DIFFERENCE

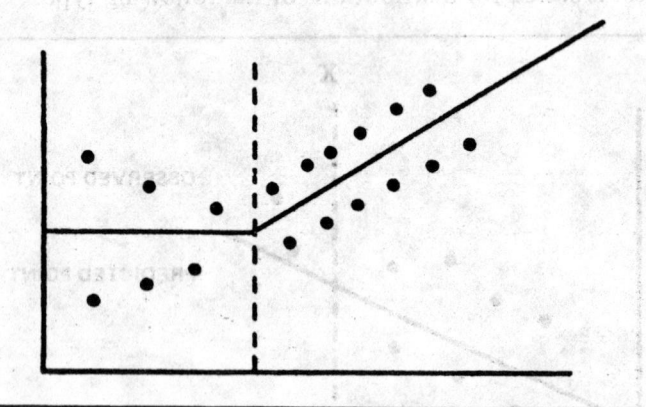

Walker-Lev Test One

This statistic evaluates the hypothesis that a common slope fits both pre-X and post-X data. This condition (i.e., a common slope) may hold even if the occurrence of an event causes a change in the mean level at which the series operates, e.g., a five-year plan may result in a shift in productivity to higher levels without affecting the rate of economic growth.

Walker-Lev Test Three

This test yields an F-statistic which tests the null hypothesis that a common regression line fits both pre-X and post-X distributions. Separate regression estimates are calculated for both sets of data. These are subsequently compared to see if they could have been drawn from the same population.

APPENDIX II

SAMPLE CODE SHEET

```
                                              Page    /column
Date of Event              Month____Day____Year____
Location                   _____
Formations Involved        _____
Magnitude:                 _____  _____  _____
Duration_____(in days)
Intensity:
Injuries_____Property Damage_____Deaths____Arrests_____
```

Initiator of Attack

Pro-System_____(Reaction____Repression____)

Clashes_____ Anti-System_____

Ranking System

Governmental
- 11 Federal
- 12 State
- 13 Local
- 14 (Other)

Racial
- 21 White
- 22 Black
- 23 Indian
- 24 Oriental

Economic
- 31 Employer
- 32 Landlords
- 33 Credit
- 34 Commodity
- 35 Small Business
- 36 Farmer
- 37 Employees
- 38 Agricultural Laborers
- 39 Unemployed

Ethnic	41	Northern European
	42	Southern European
	43	Eastern European
	44	Latin
	45	Asian
Political Org.	51	Republican
	52	Democrat
	53	Right Wing
	54	Left Wing
	55	Anti-War
	56	Women
	57	(Other)
Religious	61	Protestant
	62	Catholic
	63	Jewish
	64	(Other)
Educational	71	University Ad.
	72	Faculty
	73	Students
	99	No Information

<u>Issue Area</u>

1. Foreign Policy
2. Racial
3. Economic
4. Religious
5. Ethnic
6. Ideological
7. Educational
9. No Information

Economic (3)
Social (2, 4, 5, 7)
Political (1, 6)

APPENDIX III
STATISTICAL DATA

Appendix III

Table III.1: Domestic Violence by Year

Year	Pro-System DE	DU	AR	#	Clashes DE	DU	AR	#	Anti-System DE	DU	AR	#	Reaction DE	DU	AR	#	Totals DE	DU	AR	#
1890	0	1	2	1	2	13	0	12	0	1	0	1					2	15	2	14
1891	0	1	17	1	4	22	36	16	0	0	0	0					4	23	53	17
1892	0	2	3	2	14	21	2	21	0	0	0	0					14	23	5	23
1893	0	0	0	0	27	17	0	14	0	1	0	1					27	18	0	15
1894	0	2	1	2	22	80	2	47	0	8	0	2					22	90	3	51
1895	0	0	0	0	28	32	9	20	0	0	0	0					28	32	9	20
1896	0	0	0	0	6	16	0	11	0	0	0	0					6	16	0	11
1897	0	0	0	0	41	24	0	21	0	0	0	0					41	24	0	21
1898	0	0	0	0	28	41	0	18	0	0	0	0					28	41	0	18
1899	0	0	0	0	22	44	0	20	0	0	0	0					22	44	0	20
1900	0	2	0	2	17	37	0	19	0	0	0	0					17	39	0	21
1901	0	2	4	2	7	30	14	25	0	1	0	1					7	33	18	28
1902	0	4	1	4	139	65	0	54	0	2	0	2					139	71	1	60
1903	0	1	0	1	12	47	43	39	4	5	0	5					16	53	43	45
1904	0	0	0	0	25	44	2	40	25	7	0	6					50	51	2	46
1905	1	1	0	1	5	18	0	18	1	2	0	2					7	21	0	21
1906	0	0	0	0	4	18	0	14	0	0	0	0					4	18	0	14
1913	0	10	96	10	36	74	100	69	4	4	0	4					37	88	196	83
1914	0	8	35	8	0	19	2	15	4	2	0	2					4	29	37	25
1915	0	2	0	2	0	5	0	3	0	1	0	1					0	8	0	6
1916	0	4	0	4	3	23	0	20	0	1	0	1					3	28	0	25
1917	2	14	329	14	6	42	73	34	0	0	0	0					8	56	402	48
1918	1	13	359	13	4	15	30	15	0	1	0	1					5	29	389	29
1919	0	47	482	44	16	115	145	87	8	9	0	8					24	171	627	139
1920	0	19	351	19	43	69	1	62	0	7	0	7					43	95	352	88
1921	1	21	95	13	113	91	26	85	0	9	0	9					114	121	121	107
1922	4	11	301	8	98	123	17	118	3	20	0	19					105	154	318	145
1923	0	9	37	9	19	48	76	46	0	6	0	6					19	63	113	61
1935	12	16	25	16	24	34	36	30	0	1	0	1					36	51	61	47
1936	7	13	5	12	2	27	59	24	0	1	0	1					9	41	64	37
1937	8	9	0	9	11	23	13	13	0	1	0	1					19	33	13	23
1938	2	8	0	8	3	9	0	9	0	0	0	0					5	17	0	17
1939	1	4	0	4	2	8	33	8	0	0	0	0					3	12	33	12
1940	1	6	35	6	1	2	0	2	0	0	0	0					2	8	35	8
1941	0	3	7	3	0	15	0	13	0	1	0	1					0	19	7	17
1942	4	6	3	5	4	11	0	9	0	0	0	0					8	17	3	14
1943	0	17	229	16	32	33	4	13	0	1	0	1					32	51	233	30
1944	3	7	55	7	2	4	0	4	0	0	0	0					5	11	55	11
1945	0	2	0	2	0	1	0	1	0	0	0	0	0	0	0	0	0	3	0	3
1946	7	11	8	10	6	10	0	8	0	0	0	0	0	0	0	0	13	21	8	18
1947	0	11	53	9	1	4	0	3	0	0	0	0	0	0	0	0	1	15	53	12
1948	0	3	22	3	1	3	0	3	0	0	0	0	0	5	0	5	1	11	22	11
1949	0	4	0	3	2	11	14	11	0	4	14	3	1	10	0	10	3	29	28	28
1950	1	7	18	7	0	24	115	24	1	7	2	7	0	0	0	0	2	38	135	38
1951	0	8	59	8	0	7	0	7	0	0	0	0	0	10	0	9	0	25	59	24
1952	0	4	17	4	2	10	24	10	0	2	0	2	0	1	0	1	2	17	41	17
1953	0	10	54	10	0	6	62	6	0	0	0	0	1	2	0	2	1	18	116	18
1954	0	9	14	9	0	7	49	7	1	2	4	2	0	1	0	1	1	19	67	19
1955	0	0	0	0	3	7	0	7	0	1	0	1	0	4	0	4	3	12	0	12
1956	0	6	0	6	0	13	116	13	0	0	0	0	0	4	0	4	0	23	116	23
1957	0	1	0	1	0	15	9	15	0	0	0	0	0	13	0	13	0	29	9	29
1958	0	0	0	0	0	10	55	10	0	0	0	0	1	14	7	14	1	24	62	24
1959	0	0	0	0	0	1	13	13	0	3	0	3	1	5	9	5	2	21	12	21
1960	0	5	451	5	1	27	455	27	0	1	0	1	0	14	29	13	1	47	935	46
1961	0	4	0	4	0	11	411	11	0	2	129	2	0	17	25	17	0	34	565	34
1962	0	5	0	5	0	9	4	8	0	0	0	0	1	17	0	17	1	31	4	30
1963	0	26	600	21	2	58	721	48	1	3	0	3	6	20	0	20	9	107	1321	92
1964	0	13	796	11	6	74	850	57	0	9	0	8	1	29	0	26	7	125	1646	102
1965	3	14	65	14	3	45	35	37	1	10	8	9	4	21	0	21	11	90	108	81
1966	3	15	276	14	7	78	23	61	1	25	50	22	2	18	0	18	13	136	349	115
1967	2	21	328	17	69	100	1625	77	5	128	523	82	2	25	4	22	78	274	2480	198
1968	4	22	55	15	18	87	558	62	44	130	4596	89	3	11	0	11	69	250	5209	177
1969	5	22	34	22	4	57	505	48	13	108	797	79	0	1	0	1	22	188	1336	149
1970	12	13	154	12	1	24	241	21	9	47	671	38	2	8	43	7	24	92	1109	78
Totals	84	499	5476	458	949	2070	6598	1683	122	574	6794	435	25	117	250	241	1180	3393	18985	2817

Table III.2: Political Organizational Violence by Year

Year	Pro-System DE	DU	AR	#	Clashes DE	DU	AR	#	Anti-System DE	DU	AR	#	Reaction DE	DU	AR	#	Totals DE	DU	AR	#
1890		1	2	1		0		0		0		0	0				0	1	2	1
1891		1	17	1		1	1	1		0		0					0	2	18	2
1892		0		0		0		0		0		0					0	0	0	0
1893		0		0	15	1		1		0		0					15	1	0	1
1894		1	1	1		2		2		0		0					0	3	1	3
1895		0		0		1		1		0		0					0	1	0	1
1896		0		0		0		0		0		0					0	0	0	0
1897		0		0		1		1		0		0					0	1	0	1
1898		0		0		0		0		0		0					0	0	0	0
1899		0		0		0		0		0		0					0	0	0	0
1900		0		0		3		3		0		0					0	3	0	3
1901		1		1		2		2		0		0					0	3	0	3
1902		0		0		1		1		0		0					0	1	0	1
1903		1		1		1		1		0		0					0	2	0	2
1904		0		0		0		0		0		0					0	0	0	0
1905		0		0		1		1		0		0					0	1	0	1
1906		0		0		1		1		0		0					0	1	0	1
1913		0		0		2		2		1		1					0	3	0	3
1914		1	2	1		1		1		1		1					0	3	3	3
1915		0		0		1		1		0		0					0	1	0	1
1916		2		2		3		3		0		0					0	5	0	5
1917		11	176	11	6	22	73	19		0		0					6	33	249	30
1918	1	11	309	11	1	5	9	5		0		0					2	16	318	16
1919		38	408	35	5	9	6	8	4	2		2					9	49	414	45
1920		15	347	15		1	1	1		1		1					0	17	348	17
1921		18	93	10		2	0	1		0		0					0	20	93	11
1922		4	301	4		1	0	1		0		0					0	5	301	5
1923		9	37	9		4		4		1		1					0	14	37	14
1935		2		2		5	6	5		1		1					0	8	6	8
1936		2	5	2		1		1		0		0					0	3	5	3
1937		0		0		1		1		0		0					0	1	0	1
1938		2		2	2	6		6		0		0					2	8	0	8
1939		1		1		2	11	2		0		0					0	3	11	3
1940		3		3		0		0		0		0					0	3	0	3
1941		2	7	2		0		0		0		0					0	2	7	2
1942		0	0	0		0		0		0		0					0	0	0	0
1943		10	233	10		0		0		0		0					0	10	233	10
1944	2	1	0	1	2	1		1		0		0					4	2	0	2
1945		1		1		0		0		0		0	0		0		0	1	0	1
1946		1	8	1		1		1		0		0	0		0		0	2	8	2
1947		3	14	3		2		1		0		0	0		0		0	5	14	4
1948		3	22	3		1		1		0		0	1		1		0	5	22	5
1949		3	0	2		2		2		0		0	0		0		0	5	0	4
1950		5	10	5		7		7	1	2	2	2	0		0		1	14	12	14
1951		8	59	8		0		0		0		0	0		0		0	8	59	8
1952		3	17	3	1	3	10	3		0		0	0		0		1	6	27	6
1953		9	18	9		0		0		0		0	0		0		0	9	18	9
1954		9	14	9		0		0	1	1		1	0		0		1	10	14	10
1955		0		0		0		0		0		0	0		0		0	0	0	0
1956		6		6		0		0		0		0	0		0		0	6	0	6
1957		0		0		0		0		0		0	0		0		0	0	0	0
1958		0		0		0		0		0		0	0		0		0	0	0	0
1959		0		0		0		0		0		0	0		0		0	0	0	0
1960		0		0		0		0		0		0	0		0		0	0	0	0
1961		1		1		1		1		0		0	0		0		0	2	0	2
1962		0		0		0		0		0		0	0		0		0	0	0	0
1963		0		0		0		0	1	1		1	0		0		1	1	0	0
1964		1	796	1		2		2		1		1	1		1		0	5	796	5
1965		3		3		8	16	8		1		1	0		0		0	12	16	12
1966		4	276	4	1	9	5	9		6		6	4		4		1	23	281	23
1967		7	237	7	1	10	80	10		5	23	5	0		0		1	22	340	22
1968		10	55	6		25	529	20	1	11		9	2		2		1	48	584	37
1969		15	34	15		26	441	19		26	298	26	0		0		0	67	773	60
1970	6	9	139	8		8	172	8	3	17	334	13	2		2		9	36	645	31
Totals	9	238	3627	221	34	187	1360	169	11	78	657	72	0	10	0	10	54	513	5644	472

Appendix III

[143]

Table III.3: Economic Violence by Year

Year	Pro-System DE	DU	AR	#	Clashes DE	DU	AR	#	Anti-System DE	DU	AR	#	Reaction DE	DU	AR	#	Totals DE	DU	AR	#
1890	0	0	0	0	0	5	0	4	0	1	0	1					0	6	0	5
1891	0	0	0	0	0	5	35	5	0	0	0	0					0	5	35	5
1892	0	2	3	2	0	9	2	9	0	0	0	0					0	11	5	11
1893	0	0	0	0	0	1	0	1	0	1	0	1					0	2	0	2
1894	0	1	0	1	2	59	2	35	0	8	0	2					2	68	2	38
1895	0	0	0	0	1	3	9	3	0	0	0	0					1	3	9	3
1896	0	0	0	0	0	12	0	7	0	0	0	0					0	12	0	7
1897	0	0	0	0	30	10	0	9	0	0	0	0					30	10	0	9
1898	0	0	0	0	14	19	0	8	0	0	0	0					14	19	0	8
1899	0	0	0	0	0	29	0	10	0	0	0	0					0	29	0	10
1900	0	1	0	1	6	21	0	5	0	0	0	0					6	22	0	6
1901	0	1	4	1	5	18	14	13	0	1	0	1					5	20	18	15
1902	0	1	1	1	14	55	0	45	0	2	0	2					14	58	1	48
1903	0	0	0	0	3	32	43	25	4	5	0	5					7	37	43	30
1904	0	0	0	0	11	32	2	29	25	7	0	6					36	39	2	35
1905	1	1	0	1	0	8	0	8	1	2	0	2					2	11	0	11
1906	0	0	0	0	0	3	0	3	0	0	0	0					0	3	0	3
1913	0	10	96	10	30	66	100	61	1	3	0	3					31	79	196	74
1914	0	7	33	7	0	17	2	13	4	1	0	1					4	25	35	21
1915	0	2	0	2	0	1	0	1	0	1	0	1					0	4	0	4
1916	0	2	0	2	1	18	0	15	0	1	0	1					1	21	0	18
1917	2	2	150	2	0	2	0	2	0	0	0	0					2	4	150	4
1918	0	2	50	2	0	2	21	2	0	0	0	0					0	4	71	4
1919	0	9	74	9	4	57	39	44	4	7	0	6					8	73	113	59
1920	0	4	4	4	7	30	0	25	0	6	0	6					7	40	4	35
1921	0	2	2	2	6	49	26	46	0	7	0	7					6	58	28	55
1922	4	7	0	4	79	97	17	92	3	20	0	19					86	124	17	115
1923	0	0	0	0	3	11	1	11	0	2	0	2					3	13	1	13
1935	0	2	25	2	24	27	30	23	0	0	0	0					24	29	55	25
1936	0	3	0	2	2	21	22	18	0	1	0	1					2	25	22	21
1937	2	3	0	3	11	21	13	11	0	1	0	1					13	25	13	15
1938	0	2	0	2	0	0	0	0	0	0	0	0					0	2	0	2
1939	0	1	0	1	2	6	22	6	0	0	0	0					2	7	22	7
1940	0	1	35	1	0	0	0	0	0	0	0	0					0	1	35	1
1941	0	0	0	0	0	15	0	13	0	1	0	1					0	16	0	14
1942	0	1	3	1	3	2	0	2	0	0	0	0					3	3	3	3
1943	0	0	0	0	0	0	0	0	0	0	0	0					0	0	0	0
1944	0	0	0	0	0	1	0	1	0	0	0	0					0	1	0	1
1945	0	0	0	0	0	0	0	0	0	0	0	0					0	0	0	0
1946	0	0	0	0	4	3	0	3	0	0	0	0					4	3	0	3
1947	0	0	0	0	0	0	0	0	0	0	0	0					0	0	0	0
1948	0	0	0	0	0	0	0	0	0	0	0	0	0	0	0	0	0	0	0	0
1949	0	0	0	0	2	7	14	7	0	4	14	4	0	0	0	0	2	11	0	11
1950	0	1	8	1	0	11	3	11	0	5	0	5	0	0	0	0	0	17	11	17
1951	0	0	0	0	0	1	0	1	0	0	0	0	0	0	0	0	0	1	0	1
1952	0	0	0	0	0	0	0	0	0	2	0	2	0	0	0	0	0	2	0	2
1953	0	1	36	1	0	3	48	3	0	0	0	0	1	1	0	1	1	5	84	5
1954	0	0	0	0	0	7	49	7	0	1	4	1	0	1	0	1	0	9	53	9
1955	0	0	0	0	2	4	0	4	0	1	0	1	0	0	0	0	2	5	0	5
1956	0	0	0	0	0	0	0	0	0	0	0	0	0	0	0	0	0	0	0	0
1957	0	0	0	0	0	0	0	0	0	0	0	0	0	0	0	0	0	0	0	0
1958	0	0	0	0	0	2	0	2	0	0	0	0	0	0	0	0	0	2	0	2
1959	0	0	0	0	1	9	3	9	0	3	0	3	0	0	0	0	1	12	3	12
1960	0	0	0	0	0	0	0	0	0	0	0	0	0	0	0	0	0	0	0	0
1961	0	0	0	0	0	0	0	0	0	0	0	0	0	0	0	0	0	0	0	0
1962	0	0	0	0	0	0	0	0	0	0	0	0	0	0	0	0	0	0	0	0
1963	0	0	0	0	0	1	0	1	0	0	0	0	0	0	0	0	0	1	0	1
1964	0	0	0	0	0	0	0	0	0	0	0	0	0	0	0	0	0	0	0	0
1965	0	0	0	0	0	0	0	0	0	0	0	0	0	0	0	0	0	0	0	0
1966	0	0	0	0	0	1	0	1	0	0	0	0	0	0	0	0	0	1	0	1
1967	0	0	0	0	0	1	0	1	0	0	0	0	0	0	0	0	0	1	0	1
1968	0	0	0	0	0	3	0	2	0	1	0	1	0	0	0	0	0	4	0	3
1969	0	0	0	0	0	1	0	1	0	0	0	0	0	0	0	0	0	1	0	1
1970	0	0	0	0	0	2	0	2	0	0	0	0	0	0	0	0	0	2	0	2
Totals	9	69	524	65	276	820	517	660	42	95	18	86	1	2	0	2	319	986	1059	813

Table III.4: Social Violence by Year

Year	Pro-System DE	DU	AR	#	Clashes DE	DU	AR	#	Anti-System DE	DU	AR	#	Reaction DE	DU	AR	#	Totals DE	DU	AR	#
1890		0		0	2	8		8		0	0						2	8	0	8
1891		0		0	4	16		10		0	0						4	16	0	10
1892		0		0	14	12		12		0	0						14	12	0	12
1893		0		0	12	15		12		0	0						12	15	0	12
1894		0		0	20	19		10		0	0						20	19	0	10
1895		0		0	27	28		16		0	0						27	28	0	16
1896		0		0	6	4		4		0	0						6	4	0	4
1897		0		0	11	13		11		0	0						11	13	0	11
1898		0		0	14	22		10		0	0						14	22	0	10
1899		0		0	22	15		10		0	0						22	15	0	10
1900		1		1	11	13		11		0	0						11	14	0	12
1901		0		0	2	10		10		0	0						2	10	0	10
1902		3		3	125	9		8		0	0						125	12	0	11
1903		0		0	9	14		13		0	0						9	14	0	13
1904		0		0	14	12		11		0	0						14	12	0	11
1905		0		0	5	9		9		0	0						5	9	0	9
1906		0		0	4	14		10		0	0						4	14	0	10
1913		0		0	6	6		6		0	0						6	6	0	6
1914		0		0	0	1		1		0	0						0	1	0	1
1915		0		0	0	3		1		0	0						0	3	0	1
1916		0		0	2	2		2		0	0						2	2	0	2
1917		1	3	1	0	18		13		0	0						0	19	3	14
1918		0		0	3	8		8	1		1						3	9	0	9
1919		0		0	7	49	100	35		0	0						7	49	100	35
1920		0		0	36	38		36		0	0						36	38	0	36
1921	1	1		1	107	40		38		2	2						108	43	0	41
1922		0		0	19	25		25		0	0						19	25	0	25
1923		0		0	16	33	75	31		3	3						16	36	75	34
1935	12	12		12		2		2		0	0						12	14	0	14
1936	7	8		8	5		37	5		0	0						7	13	37	13
1937	6	6		6	1			1		0	0						6	7	0	7
1938	2	4		4	1	3		3		0	0						3	7	0	7
1939	1	2		2	0			0		0	0						1	2	0	2
1940	1	2		2	1	2		2		0	0						2	4	0	4
1941		1		1	0			0		0	0						0	1	0	1
1942	4	5		4	1	9		7		0	0						5	14	0	11
1943		7	6	6	32	33	4	13	1		1						32	41	10	20
1944	1	6	55	6		2		2		0	0						1	8	55	8
1945		1		1		1		1		0	0						0	2	0	2
1946	7	10		9	2	6		4		0	0						9	16	0	13
1947		8	39	6	1	2		2		0	0		0		0		1	10	39	8
1948		0		0	1	2		2		0	0		4		4		1	6	0	6
1949		1		1		2		2		0	0		1	10	10		1	13	0	13
1950	1	1		1	6		112	6		0	0		0		0		1	7	112	7
1951		0		0	6	6		6		0	0		10		9		0	16	0	15
1952		1		1	1	7	14	7		0	0		1		1		1	9	14	9
1953		0		0		3	14	3		0	0		1		1		1	4	14	4
1954		0		0		0		0		0	0		0		0		0	0	0	0
1955		0		0	1	3		3		0	0		4		4		1	7	0	7
1956		0		0	13	116		13		0	0		4		4		0	17	116	17
1957		1		1	15	9		15		0	0		13		13		0	29	9	29
1958		0		0	8	55		8		0	0		1	14	7	14	1	22	62	22
1959		0		0	4			4		0	0		1	5	9	5	1	9	9	9
1960		5	451	5	1	27	455	27	1	0	1		14	29	13		1	47	935	46
1961		3	0	3		10	411	10	2	129	2		17	25	17		0	32	565	32
1962		5	0	5	9	4		8	0	0	1		17	0	17		1	31	4	30
1963		26	600	21	2	57	721	47	2	0	2		6	20	0	20	8	105	1321	90
1964		12	0	10	6	72	850	55	8	0	7		1	28	0	25	7	120	850	97
1965	3	11	65	11	3	37	19	29	1	9	8	8	4	21	0	21	11	78	92	69
1966	3	11	0	10	6	68	18	51	1	19	50	16	2	14	0	14	12	112	68	91
1967	2	14	91	10	68	89	1545	66	5	123	500	77	2	25	4	22	77	251	2140	175
1968	4	12	0	9	18	59	29	40	43	118	4596	79	3	9	0	9	68	198	4625	137
1969	5	7	0	7	4	30	64	28	13	82	499	53		1	0	1	22	120	563	89
1970	6	4	15	4	1	14	69	11	6	30	337	25	2	6	43	5	15	54	464	45
Totals	66	192	1325	172	648	1063	4721	854	69	401	6119	277	24	238	117	229	807	1894		1532
																		12282		

BIBLIOGRAPHY

Baltzell, E. Digby, *Philadelphia Gentlemen: The Making of a National Upper Class.* New York: Free Press, 1958.
Bandura, Albert, "Relationship of Family Patterns to Child Behavior Disorders." *Progress Report, U.S.P.H.* Stanford University, 1960.
——— ,"Social Learning through Imitation, In M. R. Jones (ed.) *Nebraska Symposium on Motivation,* Lincoln: University of Nebraska Press, 1962, pp. 211-269.
Bandura, A., D. Lipsher and Paula E. Miller, "Psychotherapists Approach-avoidance Reactions to Patients' Expression of Hostility." *Journal of Consulting Psychology,* 1960, pp. 24, 1-8.
Bandura, A., Dorothea Ross and Sheila A. Ross, "Transmission of Aggression through Imitation of Aggressive Models." *Journal of Abnormal Social Psychology,* 1961, 63, pp. 575-582.
——— ,"Imitation of Film Mediated Aggressive Models." *Journal of Abnormal Social Psychology,* 1963, 66, pp. 3-11.
Bandura, A. and R. H. Walters, *Adolescent Aggression.* New York: Ronald, 1959.
——— , *Social Learning and Personality Development.* New York: Holt, Rinehart and Winston, 1963.
Banks, Arthur S. and Phillip M. Gregg, "Grouping Political Systems: Q Factor Analysis of *A Cross-Polity Survey.*" *American Behavioral Scientist,* 1965, 9, pp. 3-6.
Berkowitz, Leonard, *Aggression: A Social Psychological Analysis.* New York: McGraw-Hill, 1962.
——— , *Roots of Aggression.* New York: Atherton, 1969.
Berkowitz, L. and R. G. Geen, "The Stimulus Qualities of the Target of Aggression: A Further Study." *Journal of Personality and Social Psychology,* 1967, 6, pp. 364-368.
Berkowitz, L. and Edna Rawlings, "Effects of Film Violence on Inhibition Against Subsequent Aggression." *Journal of Abnormal and Social Psychology,* 1963, 66, pp. 405-412.
Bernard, Jessie, "The Sociological Study of Conflict." *The Nature of Conflict.* New York: UNESCO, 1957.
Beteille, Andre (ed.), "Introduction." *Social Inequality.* Middlesex: Penguin Books, 1969.
Binder, A., D. McConnel and Nancy A. Sjoholm, "Verbal Conditioning as a Function of Experimenter Characteristics." *Journal of Abnormal Social Psychology,* 1957, 55, pp. 309-314.
Bottomore, Thomas D., *Classes in Modern Society.* London: George Allen and Unwin, 1965.
Boulding, Kenneth, *Conflict and Defense.* New York: Harper and Row, 1962.

Boulding, Kenneth, "Toward a Theory of Peace." Fisher Roser (ed.), *International Conflict and Behavioral Science.* New York: Basic Books, 1964.

Brecher, Jeremy, *Strike.* San Francisco: Straight Arrow Books, 1972.

Brooks, Robin, "Domestic Violence and America's Wars: A Historical Interpretation." In Graham and Gurr (eds.), *Violence in America.* New York: Signet, 1969. Pp. 503-521.

Brown, Richard Maxwell, "Historical Patterns of Violence in America." In Graham and Gurr (eds.), *Violence in America.* New York: Signet, 1969. Pp. 43-80.

Buckley, Walter, *Sociology and Modern Systems Theory.* Englewood Cliffs: Prentice-Hall, 1967.

Buss, A. H., *The Psychology of Aggression.* New York: Wiley, 1961.

——— and Ann Durkee, "Conditioning of Hostile Verbalizations in a Situation Resembling a Clinical Interview." *Journal of Consulting Psychology,* 1958, 22, pp. 415-418.

Campbell, Donald and Julian Stanley, *Experimental and Quasi-Experimental Designs for Research.* New York: Rand McNally, 1963.

Caporaso, James, "Quasi-Experimental Approaches to Social Science: Perspectives and Problems." In James Caporaso and Les Roos, *Quasi-Experimental Approaches.* Evanston: Northwestern University Press, 1973.

——— and Alan Pelowski, "Economic and Political Integration in Europe: A Time-Series Quasi-Experimental Analysis." *American Political Science Review,* 1971, 65, pp. 418-433.

Cattell, Raymond, et al., "An Attempt at More Refined Definition of the Cultural Dimensions of Syntality in Modern Nations." *American Sociological Review,* 1951, XVII, pp. 408-421.

———, "The Dimensions of Culture Patterns of Factorization of National Characters." *Journal of Abnormal and Social Psychology,* 1949, XLIV, pp. 443-469.

———, "The Culture Patterns Discoverable in the Social Dimensions of Existing Nations." *Journal of Social Psychology,* 1950, XXXII.

Chadwick, Richard, "An Analysis of the Relationship of Domestic to Foreign Conflict Behavior over the Period 1955-57." Evanston: Northwestern University, 1963.

Chaffee, Zachariah, *Freedom of Speech in the United States.* Cambridge: Harvard University Press, 1941.

Collins, John, "Foreign Conflict Behavior and Domestic Disorder in Africa." Paper presented 1969 Annual Meeting of the American Political Science Association, New York, 1969.

Cook, Fred, *The Nightmare Decade.* New York: Random House, 1971.

Corning, Peter, "Biological Bases of Behavior and Some Implications for Political Science." *World Politics,* April, 1971.

Coser, Lewis A., *The Functions of Social Conflict.* New York: Free Press, 1956.

Dahrendorf, Rolf, *Class and Class Conflict in Industrial Society.* Stanford: Stanford University Press, 1959.

Dalfiume, Richard, "Beginning the Negro Revolution." In Keith Nelson (ed.), *The Impact of War on American Life.* New York: Holt, Rinehart, and Winston, 1971, pp. 144-150.

Davies, James C., "Toward a Theory of Revolution." In Berkowitz (ed.), *Roots of Aggression.* New York: Atherton, 1969, pp. 119-130.

Davis, Kingsley and Wilbert Moore, "Some Principles of Stratification." In L. Wilson and W. L. Kolb (eds.), *Sociological Analysis.* New York: Harcourt, Brace, 1949.

Bibliography

Davitz, J. R., "The Effects of Previous Training on Post-Frustrative Behavior." *Journal of Abnormal Social Psychology,* 1952, 47, pp. 309-315.

Deutsch, Karl, et al., *Political Community and the North Atlantic Alliance.* Princeton: Princeton University Press, 1957.

Dollard, J., L. Doob, N. E. Miller, and R. R. Sears, *Frustration and Aggression.* New Haven: Yale University Press, 1939.

Domhoff, William, *Who Rules America?* Englewood Cliffs: Spectrum Books, 1967.

Durkheim, Emile, *Suicide.* (Translated by George Simpson) New York: Free Press, 1951.

Easton, David, *The Political System.* New York: Alfred A. Knopf, 1953.

Eckstein, Harry, "On the Etiology of Internal Wars." *History and Theory,* 1965, IV, pp. 133-163.

———, *Internal War.* New York: Free Press, 1966.

Fanon, Frantz, *The Wretched of the Earth.* New York: Oxford University Press, 1963.

Feierabend, Ivo K. and Rosalind L. Feierabend, "Aggressive Behaviors Within Polities, 1948-1962: A Cross-National Study." *Journal of Conflict Resolution,* 1966, X, pp. 249-271.

Frankel, Joseph, *International Relations.* New York: Oxford University Press, 1964.

Freeland, Richard, *The Truman Doctrine and the Origins of McCarthyism.* New York: Alfred A. Knopf, 1972.

Fulbright, J. William, *The Crippled Giant.* New York: Vintage Books, 1972.

Galtung, Johan, "A Structural Theory of Aggression." *Journal of Peace Research,* 1964, No. 2, pp. 95-119.

———, "Violence, Peace and Peace Research." *Journal of Peace Research,* 1969, No. 3, pp. 167-191.

Gerth, H. and C. Wright Mills, *From Max Weber.* New York: Oxford University Press, 1958.

Goldman, Jeri R. "The Relation of Certain Therapist Variables to the Handling of Psychotherapeutic Events." Unpublished doctoral dissertation, Stanford University, 1961.

Graham, Hugh Davis, "The Paradox of American Violence: A Historical Appraisal." In Short and Wolfgang (eds.), *Collective Violence.* Chicago: Aldine-Atherton, 1971, pp. 201-209.

——— and Ted Gurr, *Violence in America.* New York: Signet Books, 1969.

Gurr, Ted Robert, "A Causal Model of Civil Strife, A Comparative Analysis Using New Indices." *American Political Science Review,* 1968, 62, pp. 1104-1124.

———, "A Comparative Study of Civil Strife." In Graham and Gurr (eds.), *Violence in America.* New York: Signet Books, 1969, pp. 544-596.

———, *Why Men Rebel.* Princeton: Princeton University Press, 1970.

———, "Violence, Political Revolution and Social Change." Paper prepared for a seminar on Revolution and Social Change, Pennsylvania State University, April, 1971a.

———, "Democratic Response to Political Violence in Historical Response." Paper presented to the National Programmatic Institute on the Response to Political Violence through Democratic Means, October, 1971b.

———, *Politimetrics.* Englewood Cliffs: Prentice-Hall, 1972.

Haas, Ernst and Allen Whiting, *Dynamics of International Relations.* New York: McGraw-Hill, 1956.

Haas, Ernst, "International Integration: The European and the Universal Process." *International Organization,* 15, Summer, 1961, pp. 366-392.

Hartmann, Donald, "Influence of Symbolically Modeled Instrumental Aggression and Pain Cues on Aggressive Behavior." *Journal of Personality and Social Psychology,* 1969, 11, pp. 280-288.

Hazlewood, Leo, "Externalizing Systematic Stresses, International Conflict as Adaptive Behavior." In Jonathan Wilkenfeld (ed.), *Conflict Behavior and Linkage Politics.* New York: David McKay, 1973.

Hegel, G.W.F., *The Phenomonology of Mind.* (Translated by J. Baillie) London: Routledge and Kegan Paul, 1931.

Henry, Andrew F. and James F. Short, Jr., *Suicide and Homicide: Some Economic, Sociological and Psychological Aspects of Aggression.* New York: Free Press, 1954.

Higham, John, *Strangers in the Land.* New York: Athenum, 1967.

Hoffman, Stanley, *The State of War.* New York: Praeger, 1965.

Hofstadter, Richard, "Reflections on Violence in America." In Richard Hofstadter and Michael Wallace (eds.), *American Violence.* New York: Random House, 1970. Pp. 3-43.

Hovland, C. and R. Sears, "Minor Studies in Aggression: VI Correlation Lynchings with Economic Indices." *Journal of Psychology,* 1940, 9, pp. 301-310.

Huntington, Samuel, *Political Order in Changing Societies.* New Haven: Yale University Press, 1968.

Jackson, Elton and Richard Curtis, "Conceptualization and Measurement in the Study of Social Stratification." In H. Blalock and A. Blalock (eds.), *Methodology in Social Research.* New York: McGraw-Hill, 1968. Pp. 112-149.

Janowitz, Morris, "Patterns of Collective Racial Violence." In Graham and Gurr (eds.), *Violence in America.* New York: Signet Books, 1969, pp. 393-422.

Jenkins, Robin, "Ethnic Conflict and Class Consciousness: A Case Study from Belgium." *IPRA Studies on Peace Research,* Third Conference, Van Gorcum, Assen, 1969, Volume 3, pp. 122-137.

Kolko, Gabriel, *The Roots of American Foreign Policy.* Boston: Beacon Press, 1969.

Larder, Diane, "Effects of Aggressive Story Content on Non-Verbal Behavior." *Psychological Reports,* 1962, 11, 14.

Lasswell, Harold, *Politics.* Cleveland, Ohio: World, 1958.

Lee, J. S., "The Periodic Recurrence of Internecine Wars in China." *China Journal of Science and Arts,* 1931, XIV, pp. 111-116.

Levy, Sheldon, "A 150 Year Study of Political Violence in the United States." In Graham and Gurr (eds.), *Violence in America.* New York: Signet Books, 1969. Pp. 81-92.

Link, Arthur, *American Epoch: A History of the United States Since the 1890's.* Third Edition. New York: Alfred A. Knopf, 1966.

Lovaas, O. I., "Effect of Exposure to Symbolic Aggression on Aggressive Behavior." *Child Development,* 1961a, 32, pp. 37-44.

———, "Interaction between Verbal and Non-Verbal Behavior." *Child Development,* 1961b, 32, pp. 329-336.

McCormick, David, "A Field Theory of Dynamic International Processes." Research Report No. 40, Dimensionality of Nations Project, 1970.

Bibliography

Milgram, Stanley, "Behavioral Study of Obedience." *Journal of Abnormal Social Psychology*, 1963, 67, pp. 379-387.

Mintz, A., "A Re-Examination of Correlations between Lynchings and Economic Indices." *Journal of Abnormal Social Psychology*, 1946, 41, pp. 159-160.

Mussen, P. H. and E. Rutherford, "Effects of Aggressive Cartoons on Childrens' Aggressive Play." *Journal of Abnormal Social Psychology*, 1961, 62, pp. 461-464.

Nardin, Terry, *Theories of Conflict Management*. Peace Research Reviews, Oakville, 1971.

Nelson, Keith (ed.), *The Impact of War on American Life*. New York: Holt, Rinehart and Winston, 1971.

North, Robert, "Problems of Conflict and Integration." In Morton Kaplan (ed.), *New Approaches to International Relations*. New York: St. Martins Press, 1968.

Parsons, Talcott, *The Social System*. New York: Free Press, 1951.

———, "A Revised Analytical Approach to the Theory of Social Stratification." In R. Bendix and S. M. Lipset (eds.), *Class, Status and Power*. Glencoe: Free Press, 1953, pp. 192-228.

Patterson, G. R., M. Ludwig and Beverely Sonoda, "Reinforcement of Aggression in Children." Unpublished manuscript, University of Oregon, 1961.

Peterson, Harold C. and Roland Fite, *Opponents of War 1917-1918*. Madison: University of Wisconsin Press, 1957.

Phillips, Warren, "The Conflict Environment of Nations: A Study of Conflict Inputs to Nations in 1963." Research Report No. 42, Dimensionality of Nations Project, 1970.

Popper, Karl, *Conjectures and Refutations*. New York: Harper Torchbooks, 1968.

Quarles, Benjamin, *The Negro in the Making of America*. New York: Collier Books, 1964.

Rogowski, Ronald and Lois Wasserspring, "Does Political Development Exist—Corporatism in Old and New Societies." *Sage Professional Papers in Comparative Politics*, 3, 1972.

Rose, Richard, *Governing without Consensus! An Irish Perspective*. London: Faber and Faber Ltd., 1971.

Rosecrance, Richard, *Action and Reaction in World Politics*. Boston: Little Brown, 1963.

Rosenau, James, "Internal War as an International Event." In Rosenau (ed.), *International Aspects of Civil Strife*. Princeton: Princeton University Press, 1964, pp. 45-91.

———, *Of Boundaries and Bridges*. Princeton: Center for International Studies, 1967.

———, *Linkage Politics*. New York: Free Press, 1969.

Rummel, R. "Dimensions of Conflict Behavior within and between Nations." *General Systems Yearbook*, 1963, XIII, pp. 1-50.

———, "A Status-Field Theory of International Relations." Research Report No. 50, Dimensionality of Nations Project, August, 1971.

Schattschneider, E. E., *The Semi-Sovereign People*. New York: Holt, Rinehart and Winston, 1960.

Schelling, Thomas C., *The Strategy of Conflict*. Cambridge, Mass.: Harvard University Press.

Sears, R. R., Eleanor Maccoby, and H. Levin, *Patterns of Child Rearing.* New York: Harper, 1957.

Sears, R. R., J.A.M. Whiting, V. Howliss, and Pauline Sears, "Some Child Rearing Antecedents of Aggression and Dependency in Young Children." *Gentic Psychology, Monographs,* 1953, 47, pp. 135-234.

Seechrest, Lee, *Personal Communication.* March, 1971.

Siegel, Alberta, "Film Mediated Fantasy Aggression and Strength of Aggressive Drive." *Child Development,* 1956, 27, pp. 365-378.

Simkins, L., "Effects of Examiner Attitudes and Type of Reinforcement on the Conditioning of Hostile Verbs." *Journal of Personality,* 1961, 29, pp. 380-395.

Simmel, Georg, *Conflict and the Web of Group Affiliations.* (Translated by Kurt Wolff and Reinhard Bendix.) New York: Free Press, 1955.

Singer, J. David and Melvin Small, *The Wages of War.* New York: John Wiley and Sons, 1972.

Sorokin, P., "Social and Political Dynamics." Vol. III. *Fluctuations of Social Relationships, War and Revolution.* New York: American Book Company, 1937.

Staples, F. R. and R. H. Walters, "Influence of Positive Reinforcement of Aggression on Subjects Differing in Initial Aggression Level." *Journal of Consulting Psychology,* 1964, 28, pp. 547-572.

Steel, Ronald, "The Power and Old Glory." *New York Review of Books,* May, 1973, XX, Number 9, pp. 29-34.

Stevenson, Hugh Michael, "Conflict and Instability in Africa." Ph.D. dissertation, Northwestern University, 1971.

Stohl, M., "The Study of Conflict Behavior within and between Nations: Some New Evidence." Paper presented to the Annual Meetings of the Midwest Political Science Association, May, 1971.

Sumner, William Graham, *Folkways.* Boston: Ginn, 1906.

Sween, Joyce and Donald T. Campbell, "A Study of the Effect of Proximally Autocorrelated Error on Tests of Significance for the Interrupted Time-Series Quasi-Experimental Design." Department of Psychology, Northwestern University, Mimeo, 1965.

Taft, Philip and Philip Ross, "American Labor Violence: Its Causes, Character and Outcome." In Graham and Gurr (eds.), *Violence in America.* New York: Signet Books, 1969, pp. 270-376.

Tanter, R., "Dimensions of Conflict Behavior within and between Nations." Ph.D. dissertation. Bloomington: Indiana University, 1964.

———, "Dimensions of Conflict Behavior within and between Nations, 1958-1960." *Journal of Conflict Resolution,* March, 1966, X, pp. 41-64.

Tilly, Charles, "Collective Violence in European Perspective." In Graham and Gurr (eds.), *Violence in America.* New York: Signet Books, 1969, pp. 4-42.

deTocqueville, Alexis, *Democracy in America.* Volume 2. New York: Vintage Books, 1954.

Tonnies, Ferdinand, *Community and Society: Gemeinschaft und Gesellschaft.* (Translated and edited by Charles P. Loomis.) (New York: Harper Torchbooks, 1963.

Walters, R. H. and M. Brown, "Studies of Reinforcement of Aggression: III Transfer of Responses to an Interpersonal Situation." *Child Development,* 1963, 34, pp. 207-214.

Walters, R. H. and J. Thomas, "Enhancement of Punitiveness by Visual and Audiovisual Displays." *Canadian Journal of Psychology,* 1963, 17, pp. 244-255.

Bibliography

Walters, R. H., J. Thomas and W. Acker, "Enhancement of Punitive Behavior by Audio-visual Displays." *Science,* 1962, 136, pp. 872-873.

Warner, Lloyd and Paul Lunt, *The Social Life of a Modern Community.* New Haven: Yale University Press, 1941.

Weber, Max, *The Theory of Social and Economic Organizations.* (Translated by Talcott Parsons.) New York: Free Press, 1947.

Wiley, Norbert, "America's Unique Class Politics: The Interplay of the Labor, Credit and Commodity Markets." In Hans Peter Drertzel (ed.), *Recent Sociology.* New York: Macmillan, 1969. Pp. 187-213.

Wilkenfeld, J. "Domestic and Foreign Conflict Behavior of Nations." *Journal of Peace Research,* 1968, I, pp. 56-69.

———, "Research Communication: Some Further Readings Researching the Domestic and Foreign Conflict Behaviors of Nations." *Journal of Peace Research,* 1969, pp. 147-155.

——— (ed.), *Conflict Behavior and Linkage Politics.* New York: David McKay, 1973.

Wilkenfeld, J. and D. Zinnes, "A Linkage Model of Domestic Conflict Behavior." In Wilkenfeld (ed.), *Conflict Behavior and Linkage Politics,* 1973, pp. 325-356.

Williams, William A., *The Roots of the Modern American Empire.* New York: Vintage Books, 1970.

Wright, Quincy, *A Study of War.* Chicago: University of Chicago Press.

Zadek, Meira E., "The Conditioning of Verbal Behavior with Negative Cultural Connotations." *Journal of Personality,* 1959, 27, pp. 477-486.

ABOUT THE AUTHOR

MICHAEL STOHL is Assistant Professor in the Department of Political Science at Purdue University, in Lafayette, Indiana, and concurrently serves as a Research Associate at the Richardson Institute for Conflict and Peace Research, in London. He has studied at the State University of New York at Buffalo and at Northwestern University, where he received his Ph.D. His publications include "Alternative Future for Peace Research," which appeared in the *Journal of Conflict Resolution,* and the chapter entitled "Linkages Between War and Domestic Violence in the United States 1890-1923: A Quasi-Experimental Analysis," which appeared in *Quasi-Experimental Approaches,* edited by James A. Caporaso and Leslie Roos. The present volume is his first book.

55 132